Touring Atlas
SCOTLAND

BARTHOLOMEW

Published by
Bartholomew
Duncan Street
Edinburgh EH9 1TA

ISBN 0 7028 0972 1

Printed by Bartholomew in Edinburgh, Scotland

B/N 2950

Touring Atlas
SCOTLAND

CONTENTS

Map Legend 4

Key to Map Pages 5

Touring Maps 6

Tourist Information
Centres in Scotland 41

Places of Interest 43

Index to Place Names 53

BARTHOLOMEW

Legend

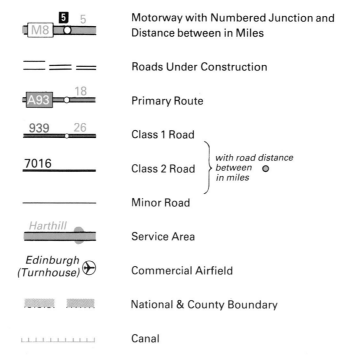

5 5 M8	Motorway with Numbered Junction and Distance between in Miles
	Roads Under Construction
A93 18	Primary Route
939 26	Class 1 Road
7016	Class 2 Road
	Minor Road
Harthill	Service Area
Edinburgh (Turnhouse)	Commercial Airfield
	National & County Boundary
	Canal

with road distance between in miles ○

SCALE 1:316,800 5 miles to 1 inch

Miles 0 1 2 3 4 5   10   15 Miles

Kms. 0 2 4 6 8   16   24 Kms.

Tourist Information Legend

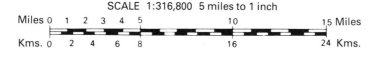

Tourist Information Centre	Horse Racing
Castle	Motor Sport
Historic House	Skiing
Cathedral, Abbey, Church	Mountain Rescue Station
Garden/Botanical Garden	Picnic Site
Museum/Art Gallery	Youth Hostel
Ancient Monument, Monument	Camping/Caravan Site
Zoo, Wildlife Park	Leisure Centre
Bird Sanctuary/Nature Reserve	Pleasure Steamer
Nature Trail, Forest Park	Vehicle Ferry
Country Park	Passenger Ferry
Other Tourist Feature	Lighthouse
Riding/Pony Trekking	Windmill
Nine Hole Golf Course	Sandy Beach
Eighteen Hole Golf Course	Wood, Forest

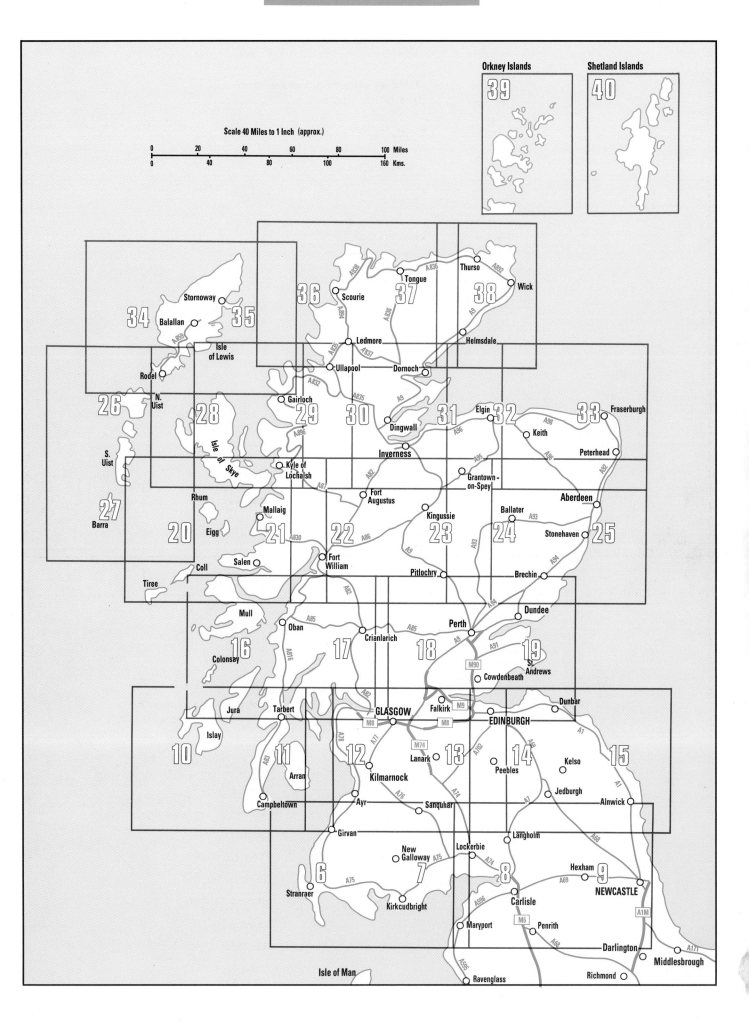

Orkney Islands

39

Shetland Islands

40

Scale 40 Miles to 1 Inch (approx.)

0   20   40   60   80   100 Miles
0   40   80   100   160 Kms.

Stornoway

34   35

Balallan

Isle
of Lewis

Scourie

36

Tongue

37

Thurso

38

Wick

Ledmore

Helmsdale

Rodel

26

N.
Uist

Ullapool

Dornoch

Gairloch

28   29   30

31

Elgin

32

Fraserburgh

33

Dingwall

Keith

Peterhead

S.
Uist

Isle
of Skye

Inverness

Grantown-
on-Spey

Kyle of
Lochalsh

Rhum

Fort
Augustus

Aberdeen

Mallaig

Kingussie

Ballater

27

20   21   22   23   24   25

Barra

Eigg

Stonehaven

Salen

Fort
William

Coll

Pitlochry

Brechin

Tiree

Mull

Dundee

Oban

Perth

Colonsay

16   17   18   19   St
Andrews

Crianlarich

Cowdenbeath

Jura   Tarbert   GLASGOW   Falkirk   Dunbar

EDINBURGH

Islay

10   11   12   13   14   15

Arran

Lanark   Peebles   Kelso

Kilmarnock

Campbeltown   Ayr   Sanquhar   Jedburgh   Alnwick

Girvan   Langholm

New
Galloway   Lockerbie

Hexham

6   7   8   9

Stranraer   Carlisle   NEWCASTLE

Kirkcudbright   Maryport   Penrith   Darlington

Middlesbrough

Isle of Man   Ravenglass   Richmond

< Back **SEND TO PRINTER**

Print Options

GB

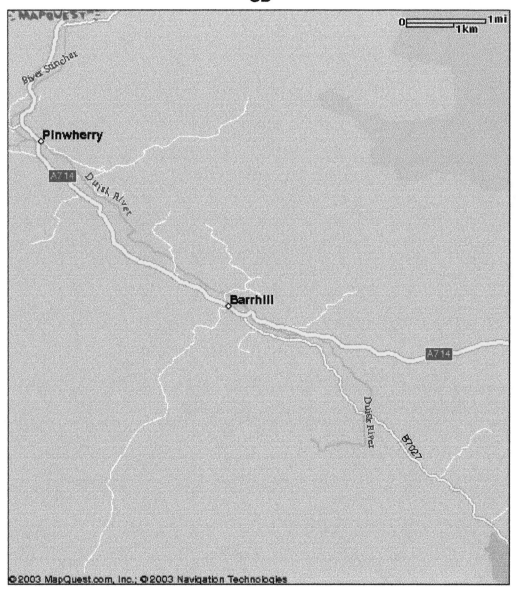

This map is informational only. No representation is made or warranty given as to its content. User assumes all risk of use. MapQuest and its suppliers assume no responsibility for any loss or delay resulting from such use.

VALITY

www.mapquest.com

GB

Print Options

Pinwherry

Duisk River

Barrhill

Duisk River

© 2003 MapQuest.com, Inc.; © 2003 Navigation Technologies

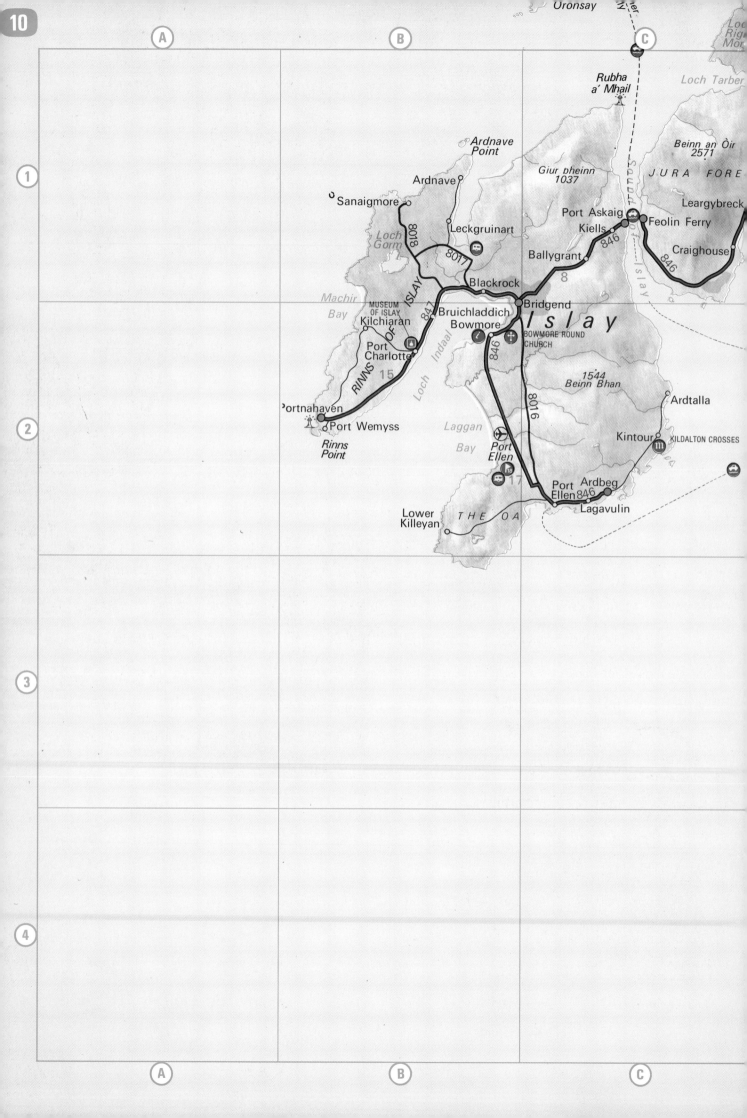

Oronsay

Loch Rig... Mor

Loch Tarber

Rubha a' Mhail

Beinn an Òir 2571

JURA FORE

Ardnave Point

Giur bheinn 1037

Ardnave

Leargybreck

Sanaigmore

Leckgruinart

Port Askaig

Feolin Ferry

Loch Gorm

8018

Kiells

846

Craighouse

8017

Ballygrant

846

Blackrock

8

Machir Bay

MUSEUM OF ISLAY

Bridgend

Islay

Kilchiaran

847

Bruichladdich

Bowmore

BOWMORE ROUND CHURCH

Port Charlotte

RINNS

OF ISLAY

15

846

1544 Beinn Bhan

Loch Indaal

8016

Ardtalla

Portnahaven

Port Wemyss

Laggan

Bay

Kintour

KILDALTON CROSSES

Rinns Point

Port Ellen

17

Port Ellen

Ardbeg

846

Lagavulin

Lower Killeyan

THE OA

D E F

1

rnspath
BOUR
FAST CASTLE (ruins)
ST. ABB'S HEAD
NATIONAL NATURE RESERVE
N.T.S.
St. Abbs
COLDINGHAM
PRIORY (ruins)
1107
22
Coldingham
21
wood
6438
Eyemouth
Cairncross
EYEMOUTH
MUSEUM
Reston
AYTON CASTLE
Ayton
Burnmouth
Auchencrow
6355
A1
arygold
6437
M NORMAN ARCH
Chirnside
Lamberton
Foulden
55
6105
nsidebridge
on
Allanton
Paxton
MANDERSTON
ackadder
TATUE
6460
Fishwick
Whitsome
6461
LADY
KIRK

BERWICK-UPON-TWEED

Tweedmouth
UNION
SUSPENSION
BRIDGE
East
Ord
Scremerston

2

6
vinton
6461
6437
6112
imprim
ESTEAD MUS.
Lane
HIRSEL
Lennel
ream
Cornhill-
on-Tweed
MARJORIBANKS
MONUMENT
Wark
am
OBELISK
Crookham
Ford
Etal
6353
Duddo
6354
Ancroft
A1
West
Allerdean
Norham
698
6525
West
Mains
Beal
West Kyloe
Fenwick
6353
Lowick
Holy Island
Holy
Island

Farne
Islands

6351
Flodden
Howtel
6352
Milfield
Mindrum
A697
Akeld
Kirknewton
Buckton
17
Middleton
Doddington
Belford 1342
Waren
Mill
Budle
Bamburgh
1340
Outchester
Glororum
Seahouses
1341
6349
Bellshill
Adderstone
Beadnell

3

KIRK YETHOLM
Town Yetholm
Wooler
6348
Chatton
Greendikes
6348
Warenford
Beadnell
Bay
Haugh
Head
29
A1
1340
6352
Brownyside
North Charlton
Christon
Bank
Embleton
The Cheviot
2676
New
Bewick
6346
South
Charlton
6347
Charlton
Mires
1339
Craster
Eglingham
6346
Rennington
1340
Windy Gyle
2036
Powburn
Glanton
Longhoughton
Whittingham
Denwick
Alnwick
Barrowburn
Callaly
A697
Hawkhill
Lesbury
6341
Alnmouth
Shillmoor
31
A1
A1068
Alnmouth
Bay
Knowe
Lorbottle
Birling
Harbottle
Cartington
Warkworth
Holystone
Flotterton
Thropton
6341
Amble
6341
Rothbury
6344
Swarland
Acklington
Nth Togston
Rochester
6341
Hepple
Pauper-
haugh
6345
Felton
Togston
Broomhill
Longframlington
Sth Broomhill
1447
Tosson
Hill
West
Thirston
Red
Row
Druridge
Bay
9
D E F
don
dge
A697
Acklington
HARWOOD
FOREST
Forestburn
Gate
19
Widdrington
orsley
Elishaw
Longhorsley
Widdrington

4

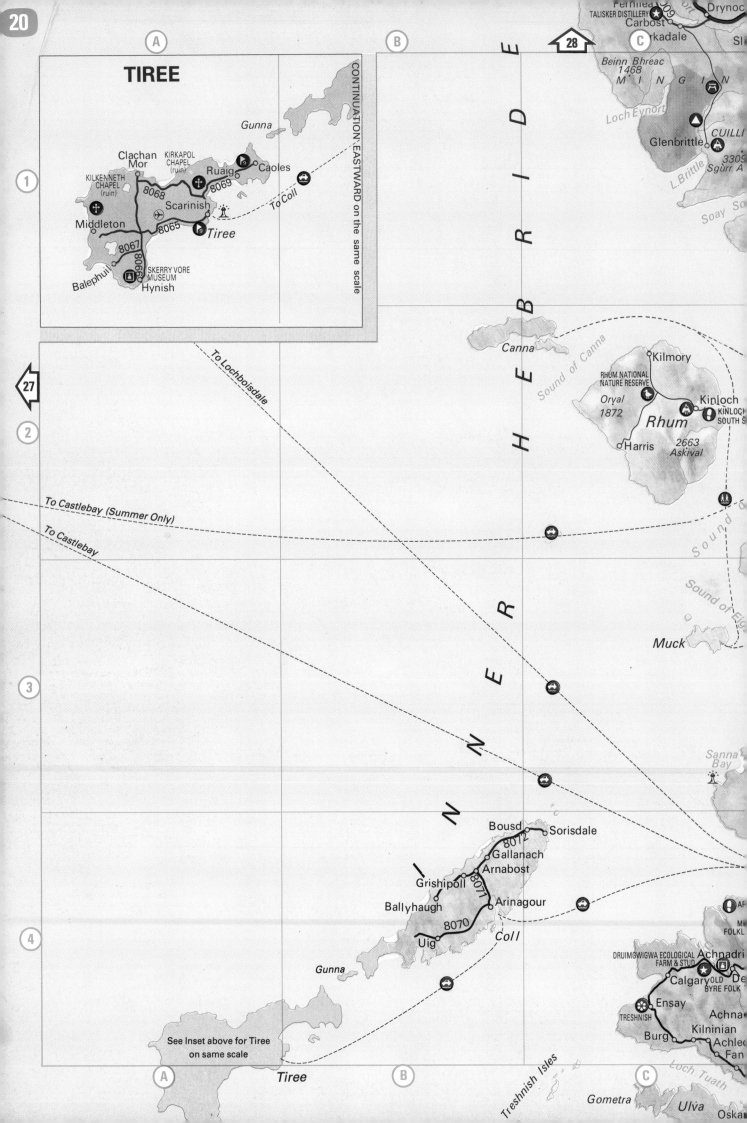

TIREE

Gunna

Clachan Mor
KIRKAPOL CHAPEL (ruin)
Ruaig
Caoles
KILKENNETH CHAPEL (ruin)
8068
8069
Scarinish
Middleton
8065
Tiree
8067
8066
Balephuil
SKERRY VORE MUSEUM
Hynish

CONTINUATION EASTWARD on the same scale

To Coll

27

28

Canna

Sound of Canna

Kilmory
RHUM NATIONAL NATURE RESERVE
Orval 1872
Kinloch
KINLOCH SOUTH S
Rhum
Harris
2663 Askival

Talisker Distillery
Carbost
rkadale
Beinn Bhreac 1468
M I N G I N
Loch Eynort
Glenbrittle
CUILLI
3309
Sgùrr A
Soay So
L. Brittle
Drynoc
Sli

H E B R I D E

I N N E R

To Lochboisdale

To Castlebay (Summer Only)

To Castlebay

2

3

Muck

Sound of Eig

Sanna Bay

Bousd
Sorisdale
8072
Gallanach
Arnabost
Grishipoll
8071
Ballyhaugh
Arinagour
8070
Uig
Coll

4

DRUIMGWIGWA ECOLOGICAL FARM & STUD
Achnadri
Calgary
OLD BYRE FOLK
Ensay
TRESHNISH
Achna
Burg
Kilninian
Achled
Fan
Loch Tuath

See Inset above for Tiree on same scale

Tiree

Gunna

Treshnish Isles

Gometra

Ulva

Oska

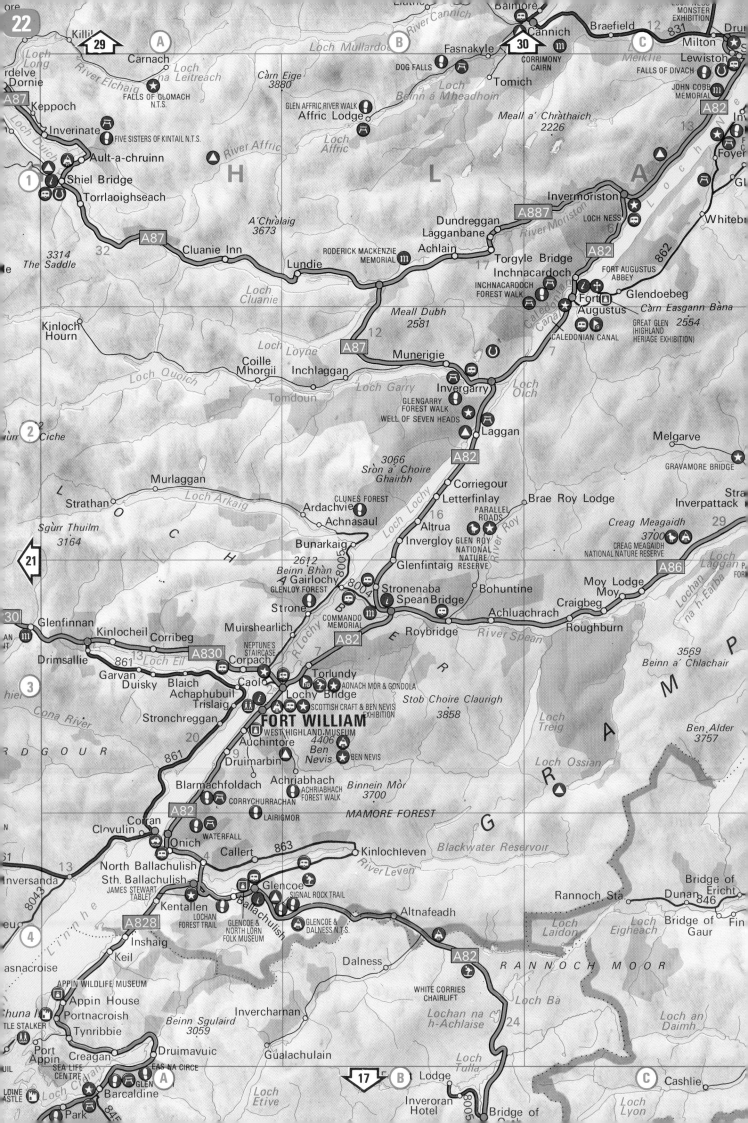

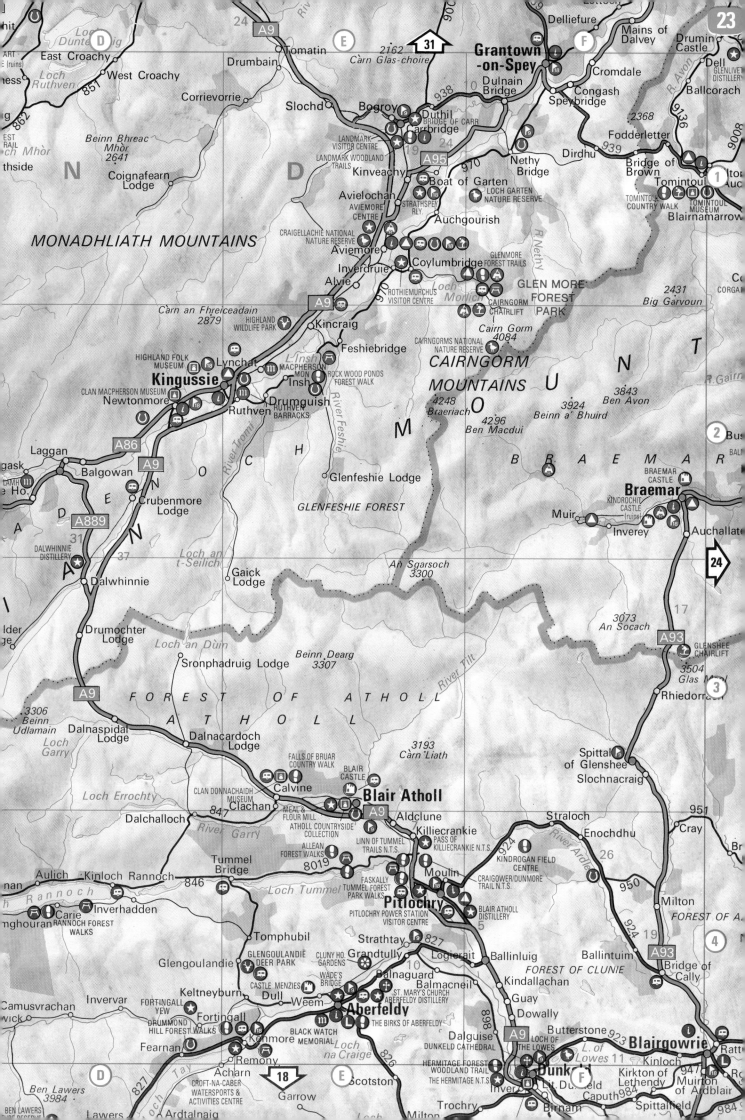

Cairnhill
FORMARTIN
Wedderlairs
TARVES MEDIEVAL TOMB
Tarves
A92
32
975
F

Pitmachie
D
LOANHEAD STONE CIRCLE
GLENGARIOCH DISTILLERY
TOLQUHON CASTLE (ruins)
33
E
Ellon
Collieston

A96
Pitcaple
Oldmeldrum
PITMEDDEN N.T.S.
Pitmedden
Bridgend
FOWLSHEUGH NATIONAL NATURE RESERVE

Kirkton of Oyne
MAIDEN STONE
MUSEUM OF FARMING LIFE N.T.S.
Kingoodie
Housieside
Newburgh

BRANDSBUTT STONE
INVERURIE MUSEUM
Whiterashes
Pettymuick
Foveran

EAST AQUHORTHIES STONE CIRCLES
Inverurie
Reisque
Rashiereive

DON VIEW
Port Elphinstone
KINKELL CHURCH (ruins)
Newmachar
Whitecairns
BALMEDIE COUNTRY PARK

ORD'S THROAT
MONYMUSK WALLED GARDEN
Kemnay
Kintore
Hatton of Fintray
Kinmundy
Balmedie

Monymusk
993
Cothall
DYCE SYMBOL STONE

Ordhead
944
Leylodge
CASTLE FRASER N.T.S.
Lyne of Skene
Blackburn
Aberdeen (Dyce)
Dyce
Stoneywood

Dunecht
9126
CRUICKSHANK BOTANIC GDN.
Bridge of Don

Echt
9119
Loch of Skene
Bucksburn
Bridge of Don

South Kirkton
of Fare
545
HAZLEHEAD
NATURE TRACKS
Westhill
Kingswells
ABERDEEN

Garlogie
Cairnie
Jessiefield
Girdle Ness

Milltown of Campfield
CULLERLIE STONE CIRCLE
KIRKHILL FOREST WALKS
Bieldside
Cults
ABERDEEN ART GALLERY
ABERDEEN MARITIME MUS.

Cullerlie
ROB ROY'S STATUE
Craigton
Nigg
(PROVOST ROSS'S HOUSE N.T.)
GORDON HIGHLANDERS' REGIMENTAL MUSEUM

DRUM CASTLE WOODLAND WALK
Milltimber
BRIDGE O' DEE
JAMES DUN'S HOUSE

Bridge of Canny
WOODLAND TRAILS
Mains of Drum
Drumoak
Peterculter
Charlestown
CAMPHILL VILLAGE TRUST

CRATHES CASTLE AND GARDENS N.T.S.
DRUM CASTLE N.T.S.
Craiglug
STORYBOOK GLEN
DUTHIE GARDENS AND WINTER GARDENS

Banchory
BANCHORY MUSEUM
Kirkton of Durris
A93
9077
979
Portlethen

Bridge of Feugh
Blairydryne
Netherley
MUCHALLS CASTLE
Cammachmore
A92

Strachan
957
Newtonhill
Muchalls

Rickarton
17

Kerloch
1747
1051
Hill of Trusta
New Mains of Ury

BURNS FAMILY TOMBSTONE AND CAIRN
STONEHAVEN
TOLBOOTH MUSEUM

Auchenblae
MEARNS FOREST WALKS
Fiddes
DUNNOTTAR CASTLE (ruins)

A94
Fordoun
10
Mill of Uras
FOWLSHEUGH SEABIRD COLONY

Howe of the Mearns
Arbuthnott
Roadside of Kinneff

Woodhead
966
Redmyre
Scotston
967
A92

9120
ARBUTHNOTT CHURCH
KINEFF OLD CHURCH

Laurencekirk
9120
Inverbervie

937
13
Johnshaven

Marykirk
St. Cyrus

North Bridge of Craigo
ST. CYRUS NATIONAL NATURE RESERVE

Hillside
Pathhead

Mains of Dun
WILLIAM LAMB MEMORIAL STUDIO
MONTROSE MUSEUM

NATURE RESERVE
MONTROSE

934
Maryton
Montrose Basin
Scurdie Ness

RED CASTLE (ruins)
Lunan Bay

Inverkeilor
14

A92
Marywell
D
E
F

ARBROATH CLIFF'S NATURE TRAIL
ARBROATH

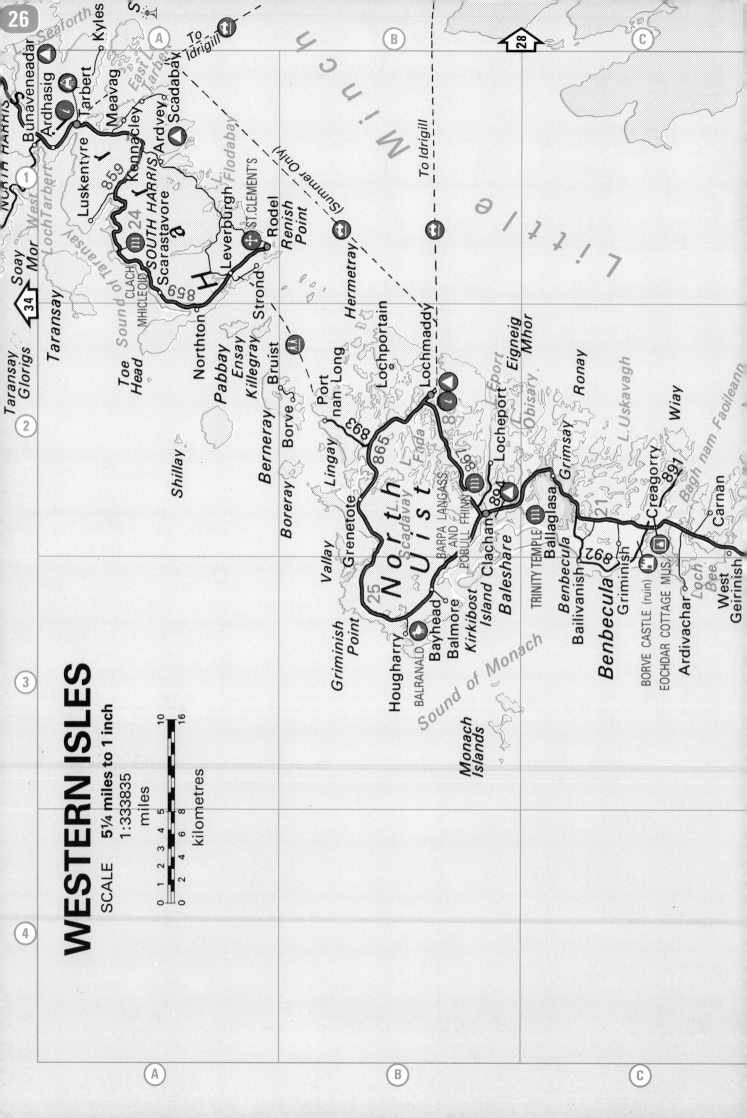

WESTERN ISLES

SCALE **5¼ miles to 1 inch**

1:333835

miles

kilometres

NORTH HARRIS

Seaforth

Kyles

Bunaveneadar

Ardhasig

Tarbert

Meavag

East Loch Tarbert

To Idrigill

Scadabay

Scadabák

LochTarbert

Soay Mor

West

Taransay Glorigs

Taransay

Sound of Taransay

Luskentyre

Kennacley

Ardvey

L. Flodabay

Leverburgh

859

SOUTH HARRIS

Scarastavore

CLACH MHICLEOID

869

ST.CLEMENT'S

Rodel

Renish Point

Toe Head

Northton

Pabbay

Ensay

Killegray

Strond

Bruist

Berneray

Borve

Shillay

Boreray

Borve

Valley

Lingay

Port nan Long

Grenetote

Griminish Point

Houghary

BALRANALD

Bayhead

Balmore

Kirkibost Island

Hermetray

Lochportain

Lochmaddy

893

865

867

894

North Uist

Scadavay

Fada

BARPA LANGASS AND POBULL FHINN

25

Clachan

Baleshare

TRINITY TEMPLE

Ballaglasa

Benbecula

Bailivanish

Griminish

BORVE CASTLE (ruin)

EOCHDAR COTTAGE MUS.

Ardivachar

West Geirinish

Locheport

Eigneig Mhor

Obisary

Grimsay

Ronay

L. Uskavagh

Bagh nam Faoileann

891

Wiay

Creagorry

892

Benbecula

21

Loch Bee

Carnan

Little Minch

Minch

Sound of Monach

Monach Islands

To Idrigill

(Summer Only)

28

34

D   E   F

1

2

3

4

D   E   F

Rudha
Hallagro

Rudha na
h-Ordaig

To Oban

To Castlebay
(Summer Only)

To Oban

Loch Eynort

Stuley

Vorran Island

Stoneybridge

ORMICLATE CASTLE
Rudha (ruin)
Ardvule

BORNISH STANDING STONE

FLORA MACDONALD'S BIRTHPLACE

Daliburgh

KILPHEDER WHEELHOUSE
North
Boisdale

Lochboisdale

Loch Boisdale

Kilbride
Roneval
·660

Sound of Eriskay

Sound of Barra

Fiaray
Eriskay

Fuday
Hellisay
Gighay

Balnabodach

SKALLARY CRAFTS

KISIMUIL CASTLE

Muldeanich

Sea

of the

Hebrides

CILLE BHARRA
CHAPEL (ruin)

Eoligarry

Greian
Head

CRAIGSTON
MUSEUM

Borve
Barra

Castlebay

Uidh

ANNIE JANE MON
Vatersay

Sandray

Pabbay

Mingulay

Berneray

Beinn Mhor
2034

Stulaval
1227

98

865

13

888
888

888

20

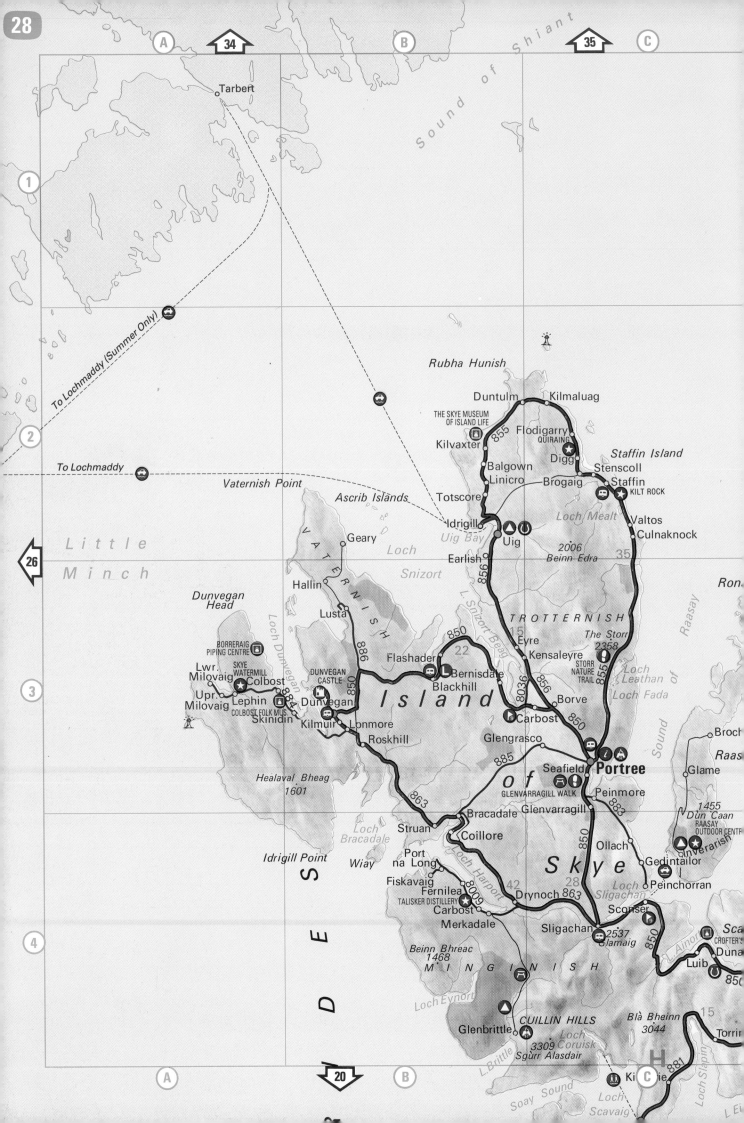

A   B   C

34

35

1

Tarbert

To Lochmaddy (Summer Only)

2

To Lochmaddy

Vaternish Point

Ascrib Islands

Sound of Shiant

Rubha Hunish

THE SKYE MUSEUM OF ISLAND LIFE

Duntulm   Kilmaluag

Kilvaxter

855

Flodigarry
QUIRAING

Digg

Balgown   Brogaig

Linicro

Staffin Island

Stenscoll
Staffin
KILT ROCK

Totscore

Idrigill

Uig Bay   Uig

Loch Mealt

Valtos
Culnaknock

Earlish

856

2006
Beinn Edra   35

Little

26

M i n c h

Loch

Snizort

L. Snizort Beag

TROTTERNISH

Raasay

Ron

Dunvegan
Head

Geary

Hallin

Lusta

V A T E R N I S H

886

850

Flashader

22

L

Bernisdale
Blackhill

Eyre

Kensaleyre

15

The Storr
2358

STORR
NATURE
TRAIL

855

Loch
Leathan

Loch Fada

BORRERAIG
PIPING CENTRE

SKYE
WATERMILL

Lwr.
Milovaig
Colbost

Upr.
Milovaig
Lephin

COLBOST FOLK MUS.

Skinidin

DUNVEGAN
CASTLE

884

Dunvegan

Kilmuir

Lonmore

Roskhill

I s l a n d

8036

856

Borve

Carbost

850

3

Healaval Bheag
1601

Glengrasco

885

Seafield
Portree

Peinmore

883

Sound of

Broch

Raas

Glame

GLENVARRAGILL WALK

o f

S k y e

Glenvarragill

Bracadale

863

Struan

Coillore

Port
na Long

Fiskavaig

Fernilea
TALISKER DISTILLERY
Carbost

Merkadale

Loch
Bracadale

Idrigill Point

Wiay

D
E
S

8009

42

28

Drynoch
863

Ollach

850

Gedintailor

Loch
Sligachan

Peinchorran

1455
Dùn Caan
RAASAY
OUTDOOR CENTRE

Inverarish

Sconser

Sligachan

2537
Glamaig

850

Sca

CROFTER'S

Duna

Luib

850

4

Beinn Bhreac
1468

M I N G I N I S H

CUILLIN HILLS

Blà Bheinn
3044

15

Glenbrittle

3309
Sgùrr Alasdair

Loch
Coruisk

L. Brittle

Torrin

881

Loch Eynort

A   B   C

20

Soay Sound

Loch
Scavaig

Ki

ie

Loch Slapin

A   38   B   C

1

at Ness

ack

2

F i r t h

Burghead   Hopeman   Covesea 9040   Branderburgh
BURGHEAD   Duffus   Lossiemouth
WELL   Cummingstown   DUFFUS   TUGNET
BURGHEAD   9013   CASTLE   ICE HOUSE   *Spey Bay*
MUS.   9012   (ruins)   INNES HOUSE   EXHIBITION
Burghead   6   OLD MILLS   GARDENS   Spey   Buckie
Bay   Newton   9103   Kingston   Bay
Findhorn   941   ELGIN   Calcots   Garmouth   Portgordon
Kinloss   Hempriggs   BAXTERS OF SPEYSIDE   Bogmuir
9089   9012   Pittendreich   VISITORS CENTRE   Portknockie   *Cullen*
Kinloss   Crook   ELGIN MUSEUM   ELGIN TOWN TRAIL   Findochty   Bay
NOS STONE   of Alves   MORAY MOTOR MUS.   Lhanbryde   A96   Portessie   FINDLATER
Springfield   A96   CATH   SPEYSIDE   A98   CASTLE
31   Forres   (ruins)   Mosstodloch   WAY   INCHGOWER   Cullen   Portsoy
PLUSGARDEN   BIRNIE CHURCH   FOLK MUSEUM   ST.NINIAN'S   DISTILLERY   LINTMILL   PORTS-
Rafford   ABBEY   Fochabers   CHAPEL   BUCKIE MARITIME   DESKFORD   COAS
DALLAS DHU   LAIGH OF MORAY   Inchberry   SPEYMOUTH FOREST   MUSEUM   CHURCH   FORDYCE
NELSON   DISTILLERY   FOREST WALKS   17   WALKS   Slackhead   (ruins)   Kirktown of
FALCONER MUS.   TOWER   Moor of Granary   9010   MILLBUIES   Forgie   Berryhillock   Deskford
RNAWAY   Kellas   COUNTRY   9103   Aultmore   Gordonstown
FOREST   Mains of   PARK   9015   Newmill   Auchinhove   Lootcherbrae
H'S LEAP   Craigmill   Dallas   13   Mulben   9018   Drumnagorrach
ugas   A941   River Lossie   River Spey   Forgie   26   Farmtown
9001   22   Newlands   9103   Blackhillock   95   Davoch of   Marnoch

3

F i r t h

23   GLEN GRANT   Crofts   12   STRATHISLA   Keith   Grange   9117
DISTILLERY   Rothes   Towiemore   DISTILLERY   Milltown   22
SECRET VALLEY WALKS   Dandaleith   CRAIGELLACHIE   Maggieknockater   Newtack   Bogniebrae
940   LADYCROFT FARM   BRIDGE   95   9115   Newton   11   Pa
CARDHU DISTILLERY   MUSEUM   9102   Craigell-   9014   Drummuir Castle   A96   Westerton   GLENDRONA
Archiestown   achie   Mains of   DISTILL
Upper Knockando   SPEYSIDE   Charlestown of   Milltown of   Cairnborrow   BRANDER MUSEUM
Cardow   WAY   Aberlour   Auchindoun   HUNTLY CASTLE
TAMDHU DISTILLERY   Speyview   BALVENIE CASTLE (ruins)   920   Huntly   (ruins)
GLENFARCLAS   Dufftown   Haugh of Glass   *S T R A T H B O G I E*
1710   DISTILLERY   A95   *Ben Rinnes*   GLENFIDDICH DISTILLERY   Dumeath
Càrn 'Kitty   Pitchroy   *2755*   DUFFTOWN   Glenfiddich   Newton
9102   Marypark   MUSEUM   Laggan   Croft
CRAGGANMORE DISTILLERY   Bellehiglash   *CLASHINDARROCH*   Culdrain
Advie   Bridge of Avon   9009   *FOREST*   Gartly   LEITH HALL &
LOCHINDORB   Lettoch   Delchirach   Eastertown   GDN. N.T.S.
CASTLE(ruins)   24   Craggan   Aultbeg   23   Bridgend   9   DRUMINNOR   PICARD
Delliefure   Mains of   Drumin   *Corryhabbie Hill*   Millton of   CASTLE   9002
939   Dalvey   Castle   *2563*   Noth   Kennethmont
4   Gra'town   Cromdale   Dell   Shenval   Rhynie   Clatt   Hardgate
-on-Spey   GLENLIVET   Tomnavoulin   Belhinnie
Dulnain   Congash   DISTILLERY   THE OLD MILL VISITOR CENTRE   Cabrach   941   Craig   97
Bridge   Speybridge   Ballcorach   *BLACKWATER FOREST*   Castle   Lumsden   Correen Hills
BR   9136   Knockandhu   *The Buck*   ST. MARY'S   1588
9008   *2368*   Fodderletter   *2368*   CHURCH   Newton   MURRAY PARK
Nethy   Dirdhu   939   CRAIG   NATURE TRAIL
Bridge   Bridge of   Milton of   *2639*   Badenyon   SCULPTURE WORKSHOPS   Mossat   Invermossat
Garten   Brown   Auchriachan   *Ladder Hills*   *G R A M*   Kildrummy
LOCH GARTEN   Tomintoul   24   KILDRUMMY CASTLE (ruins)   Milltown
NATURE RESERVE   COUNTRY WALK   Belnacraig   Bridge of
urish   TOMINTOUL   939   Mains of Glenbuchat   KILDRUMMY   Alford
Blairnamarrow   LECHT   97   CASTLE GARDENS
A   37   B   24   C

To Stromness

To Lerwick

Kinnaird Head
PITSLIGO CASTLE (ruins)
Rosehearty
Sandhaven
Fraserburgh
Fraserburgh Bay
9031
Percyhorner
Inverallochy
INVERALLOCHY
St. Combs
BANFF, WHITEHILLS & ABERCHIRDER
ST. JOHN'S CHAPEL (ruins)
Pennan
Macduff
Gardenstown
Silverford
9031
Coburty
Mid Ardlaw
9033
NFF
DUFF HOUSE
Dubford
Protstonhill
New Aberdour
Memsie
MEMSIE BURIAL CAIRN
BANFF MUSEUM
Longmanhill
Ladysford
11
A92
WRACK WOODLAND PATH
15
981
Rattray Head
EDEN CASTLE (ruins)
Keilhill
Craigmaud
CRIMONMOGATE FISHERY
enlaw
Brigend of Mountblairy
A98
New Pitsligo
17
WHITE HORSE
12
Crimond
9105
Strichen
New Leeds
18
Plaidy
Cauldwells
STRICHEN STONE CIRCLE
Blackhill
9721
Fintry
New Byth
A952
9716
9025
11
950
WHITE COW FOREST WALKS
St. Fergus
rder
Turriff
9027
956
Denhead
ADEN COUNTRY PARK & NORTH EAST OF SCOTLAND AGRICULTURAL HERITAGE CENTRE
everon
Cuminestown
B U C H A N
9024
Mains of Idoch
13
9170
Dunshillock
Mintlaw
KEITH STATUE
RUSSELL GURNEY WEAVERS
Darra
956
9029
Old Deer
Longside
Birkenhills
New Deer
Maud
DEER ABBEY (ruins)
Flushing
9 950
ortie
Mains of Towie
9170
Drymuir
Stuartfield
Millbreck
Burnhaven
Kirkton Auchterless
FYVIE CASTLE N.T.S.
Cot-town
9005
Cairnorrie
A92
PETERHEAD
Boddam
17
FYVIE CHURCH
Brownhill
12
ARBUTHNOT MUSEUM & ART GALLERY
Buchan Ness
9007
9030
Backhill
Stirling
enscoth
9992
Fyvie
Woodhead
14
Auchnagatt
Coldwells
9947
"REMAINS TO BE SEEN" MUSEUM
948
14
Auchiries
BULLERS OF BUCHAN
Rothienorman
St. Katherines
Methlick
Clola
Hatton
Fisherford
HADDO COUNTRY PARK
Toll of Birness
A952
SLAINS CASTLE (ruins)
rkton of salmond
920
HADDO HOUSE N.T.S.
Ythanbank
Cruden Bay
Cairnhill
9005
Hilton
Bogbrae
Chapel Hill
F O R M A R T I N E
Wedderlairs
TARVES MEDIEVAL TOMB
Tarves
A92
A96
Pitmachie
LOANHEAD STONE CIRCLE
GLENGARIOCH DISTILLERY
TOLQUHON CASTLE (ruins)
Ellon
32
975
Pitcaple
Oldmeldrum
Pitmedden
11
Colliston
FOWLSHEUGH NATIONAL NATURE RESERVE
Oyne
Kirkton of Oyne
MAIDEN STONE
PITMEDDEN N.T.S.
900
9170
MUSEUM OF FARMING LIFE N.T.S.
Kingoodie
Housieside
9000
Bridgend
9
Newburgh
CHIE
BRANDSBUTT STONE
Whiterashes
Pettymuick
17
Foveran
EAST AQUHORTHIES STONE CIRCLES
INVERURIE MUSEUM
Inverurie
Rashiereive
DON VIEW
947
Reisque
A92
RD'S THROAT (NIC ROUTE)
Port Elphinstone
KINKELL CHURCH (ruins)
Newmachar
979
Whitecairns
BALMEDIE COUNTRY PARK
MONYMUSK WALLED GARDEN
IE
Hatton of Fintray
919
25
Balmedie
Kemnay
Kintore
977
Cothall
DYCE SYMBOL STONE
Monymusk
9993
994
R. Don
999
Aberdeen

WESTERN ISLES

SCALE **5¼ miles to 1 inch**
1:333835

miles

0 1 2 3 4 5   10
0   2   4   6   8   16

kilometres

Flannan Isles

SI
FOLK
BLACK HOUSE
VILLAGE (ruin

East Loch Roag

Kirivick

West Loch Roag   **Croir**

Aird Uig   **Valtos**

Camas Uig   **Miavaig**   *Gt. Bernera*

Loch Roag

Uig   **Crulivig**
Geshader   STA
STC

Ardroil   8011

Loch Suainaval

Aird Brenish   **Brenish**   **Gisla**

CRAFTS   *Grunavat L*   WOODCRAFT

Loch Langavat

Mealasta Island   *Loch Resort*   **Kintara**   Ar

L   **e**

Braighe Mor   **Ardvourlie Castle**

Scarp   *Tirga Beg* 1548   *Clisham* 2622

Husinish   887   **NORTH HARRIS**

Gasker

Taransay Glorigs   *Soay Mor*   *West Loch Tarbert*   **Bunavene**
Ardhasig

Taransay   **r**

Luskentyre   859   **Tarber**

Sound of Taransay   **Meavag**

Toe Head   CLACH MHICLEOID   24   **Kennacley**
SOUTH HARRIS   **Ardvey**
Shillay   **Scarastavore**   **a**   **Scadab**

Northton   859   **H**   *L Flodabay*
Leverburgh

Pabbay   **Strond**   ST.CLEMENT'S
Ensay
Killegray   **Rodel**
Berneray   **Bruist**   **Renish Point**
Boreray   **Borve**   26   (Summ Only)

Griminish   *Valley*   *Lingay*   **Port nan Long**

Eoropie
Butt of Lewis
Five Penny Ness
ST. MOLUAG
Port of Ness
Lionel
Dell Cross
Skigersta

Five Penny
Borve
Lower Shader
Ballantrushal
CLACH AN TRUSHAL
BLACK HOUSE
Barvas
STEINACLEIT
Arnol
858
Bragar
Shawbost
way
n Bragar
857

Cellar Head

Loch
Langavat

Muirneag
808
North Tolsta
New
Tolsta

Tolsta
Head

Beinn
Mholach
955
POTTERY
Gress

Back
Upper
Coll
Coll
Tong

S
e
Newmarket
Laxdale
STORNOWAY
asclete
Eitshal
arynahine
733

Broad
Bay
866
Portnaguiran
Shulishader
Garrabost
Knock
Eye Peninsula

Sandwick
ST. COLUMBA'S
Achmore
24

f

Chicken
Head

Grimshader
Raerinish
Leurbost
Soval Lodge
Crossbost

Loch Erisort

Cromore

Laxay
Habost
Kershader
Shiltenish

Gravir
8060

W
i
S
ORINSAY
CRAFTS
P A R K
Lemreway

1874
n Mhor

Eilean
Iuyard

Loch Shell

The Minch

To Ullapool

les Scalpay

Scalpay

Sound of Shiant

Shiant Islands

To Idrigill

36

1

2

3

4

29

29

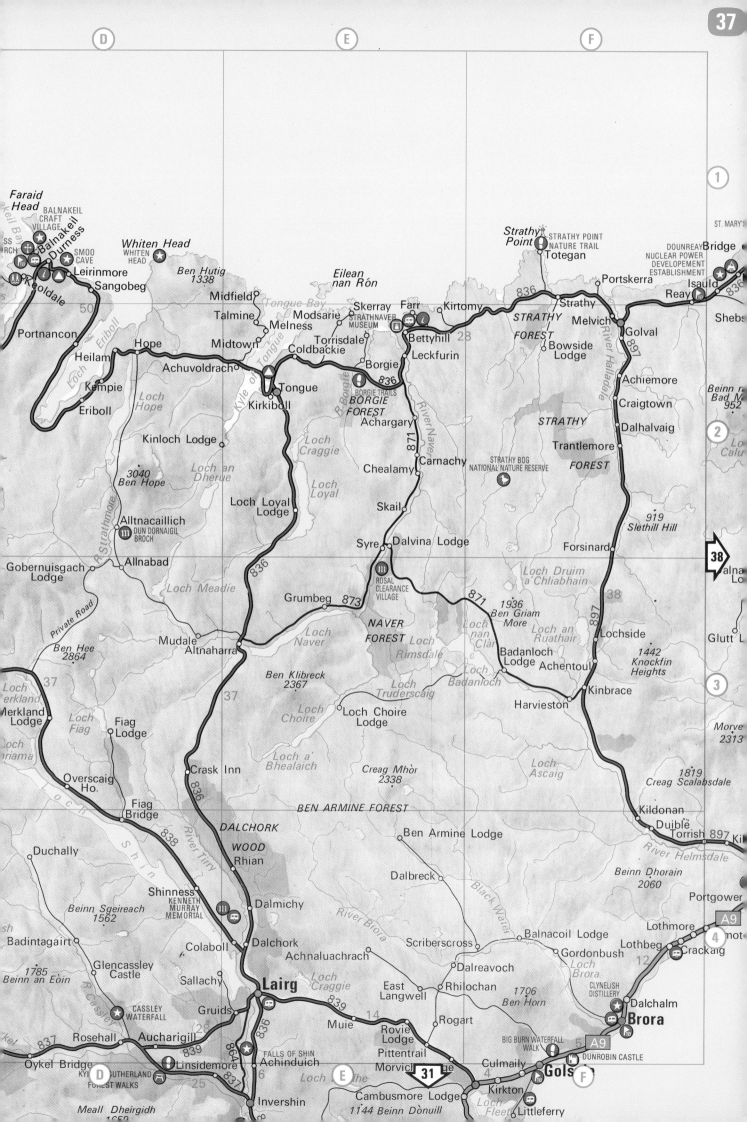

D E F

1

Faraid Head
BALNAKEIL CRAFT VILLAGE
Balnakeil Durness
SMOO CAVE
Leirinmore
Sangobeg
Portnancon
Heilam
Kempie
Eriboll
Hope
Achuvoldrach
Midtown
Kirkiboll
Tongue
Kinloch Lodge
3040 Ben Hope
Alltnacaillich
DUN DORNAIGIL BROCH
Allnabad
Gobernuisgach Lodge
Loch Meadie
Mudale
Altnaharra
Ben Hee 2864
Private Road
Merkland Lodge
Overscaig Ho.
Duchally
Fiag Bridge
Fiag Lodge
Crask Inn
DALCHORK WOOD
Rhian
Shinness
KENNETH MURRAY MEMORIAL
Beinn Sgeireach 1562
Badintagairt
Glencassley Castle
1785 Beinn an Eòin
Colaboll
Sallachy
Dalchork
Lairg
CASSLEY WATERFALL
Gruids
Rosehall
Aucharigill
Oykel Bridge
KYLE SUTHERLAND FOREST WALKS
Linsidemore
Achinduich
FALLS OF SHIN
Meall Dheirgidh 1659
Inveran
Cambusmore Lodge
1144 Beinn Dònuill

Whiten Head
WHITEN HEAD
Ben Hutig 1338
Midfield
Talmine
Melness
Torrisdale
Coldbackie
Borgie
836
BORGIE TRAILS
BORGIE FOREST
Achargary
Loch Craggie
Loch Loyal
Loch Loyal Lodge
Loch an Dherue
Loch Hope
Kyle of Tongue
Eilean nan Rón
Tongue Bay
Skerray
Modsarie
STRATHNAVER MUSEUM
Farr
Bettyhill
Leckfurin
Carnachy
Chealamy
Skail
Syre
ROSAL CLEARANCE VILLAGE
Dalvina Lodge
Grumbeg 873
NAVER FOREST
Loch Naver
Ben Klibreck 2367
Loch a' Bhealaich
Loch Choire
Loch Choire Lodge
Creag Mhòr 2338
BEN ARMINE FOREST
Ben Armine Lodge
Dalbreck
Dalmichy
Loch Craggie
Achnaluachrach
East Langwell
839
Muie 14
Rovie Lodge
Pittentrail
Morvich

Kirtomy
STRATHY FOREST
Strathy
Melvich
Golval
River Halladale
Bowside Lodge
Achiemore
Craigtown
Dalhalvaig
Trantlemore
STRATHY FOREST
STRATHY BOG NATIONAL NATURE RESERVE
919 Slethill Hill
Forsinard
Loch Druim a' Chliabhain
38
1936 Ben Griam More
Loch nan Clàr
Loch an Ruathair
Badanloch Lodge
Achentoul
1442 Knockfin Heights
Kinbrace
Harvieston
Loch Ascaig
Loch Badanloch
Loch Rimsdale
1819 Creag Scalabsdale
Kildonan
Duible
Torrish 897
River Helmsdale
Beinn Dhorain 2060
Scriberscross
Black Water
Balnacoil Lodge
Gordonbush
Loch Brora
Dalreavoch
Rhilochan
1706 Ben Horn
CLYNELISH DISTILLERY
Dalchalm
Brora
BIG BURN WATERFALL WALK
Rogart
A9
Culmaily
DUNROBIN CASTLE
Gols
Kirkton
Loch Fleet
Littleferry

Strathy Point
STRATHY POINT NATURE TRAIL
Totegan
Portskerra
DOUNREAY NUCLEAR POWER DEVELOPEMENT ESTABLISHMENT
Isauld
Reay
Shebs
ST. MARY'
Bridge
836
River Halladale
897
Portgower
A9
Lothmore
Lothbeg
Crackaig 12

38

Glutt L
Lo Calu
Morve 2313
Kin

2

3

4

ORKNEY ISLANDS

SCALE 6½ miles to 1 inch
1:411840

miles
0 1 2 4 6 8 10

kilometres
0 2 4 8 12 16

Location Map

LOCATION MAP

SHETLAND ISLANDS

Foula

Fair Isle
(not shown)

ORKNEY ISLANDS

NEW LIGHTHOUSE
Dennis Head
OLD BEACON
North Ronaldsay
Hollandstoun
HOLLAND HOUSE
BROCH OF BURRIAN
North Ronaldsay Firth

Mull Head
Papa Westray
NORTH HILL
Papa Sound
Gayfield
ST. TREDWELL'S CHAPEL

Noup Head
Rackwick
NOUP CLIFFS
Pierowall
Westray
NOTLAND CASTLE
Midbea
CROSSKIRK (ruins)
Rapness
Red Head
The North Sound
Calf of Eday

ORKNEY ANGORA
Scar
Sandquoy
Otters Wick
Sanday
Start Point
Roadside
SANDAY KNITWEAR
Kettletoft
Tres Ness
Els Ness
QUOYNESS
Braeswick
9068
9069
9070

CARRICK HO.
Carrick
CRAFTS
Faray
Millbounds
Eday
Backaland
Spur Ness
Eday Sound
Sanday Sound

Sacquoy Head
Saviskaill Bay
SWANNAY
BROUGH CHEESE MAKING EYNHALLOW CH.
OF BIRSAY (by appt.) (ruins)
Wasbister
Rousay
Eynhallow
Banks
TRUM LAND
Skaill
Egilsay
Westness
Brinyan
ST. MAGNUS
Muckle Green Holm
PIER
Wyre
CUBBIE ROO'S CASTLE (ruins)
Gairsay
Ness
9064

Brough Head
Boardhouse MILL
EARL'S PALACE (ruin)
BIRSAY MOORS
Georth
GURNESS BROCH
CLICK MILL
KIRBUSTER FM. MUS.
MARWICK HEAD
THE LOONS
Scarwell
Dounby
CORRIGALL FM. MUS.
HARRAY POTTERY
Milldoe 735
9057
9056
13
24
966

Papa Stronsay
Whitehall
ORKNEY TWEEDS
Stronsay
Samsonslane
VAT O' KIRBISTER
Millgrip
Holland
Bay of Holland
9062
9061
9060

SKARA BRAE
YESNABY SEA STACKS
Neban Point
MAES HOWE
STONES OF STENNESS
MILL
Loch of Stenness
9055
19
961
965

ELWICK MILL
Balfour
Shapinsay
Sandgarth
9058
9059
Veantrow Bay
Shapinsay Sound
Auskerry Sound
Auskerry

To Lerwick

Finstown
RENNIBISTER
CUWEEN HILL
WIDEFORD HILL
KIRKWALL
ST. MAGNUS CATH.
LOGIN'S WELL
Stromness
KNOWE OF ONSTONSTON
Loch of Kirbister
964
Wide Firth
Rerwick Head
Mull Head
BROUGH OF DEERNESS
THE GLOUP
Deer Sound
960
9050
9051
Gritley

Graemsay
Hoy Sound
Swanbister
OPHIR ROUND CHURCH (ruins)
Scapa Flow
DISTILLERY
CRAFTS LIBRARY
Quoyburray
NORWOOD MUSEUM
St Marys
ITALIAN CHAPEL
Rose Ness
967
9052
Copinsay

St John's Head
Orgill
Old Man of Hoy
Rora Head
Rackwick
DWARFIE STANE
Hoy
NAVAL BASE
Lyness
9047
Cava
Fara
Flotta
Hunda
Burray
CHURCHILL BARRIERS
8
Bring Deeps

Longhope
Saltness
Tor Ness
MELSETTER HOUSE
South Walls
Wyng
MARTELLO TOWER
Swithe
Uppertown
Bow
Herston
St Margarets Hope
OLD SMIDDY MUS.
WIRELESS MUS.
CRAFTS
South Ronaldsay
Halcro Head
9044
9043
9042
9041
9045
196
7

Swona
Burwick Cleat
TOMB OF EAGLES
To Aberdeen

Pentland Firth
Island of Stroma
Pentland Skerries

ster
Thurso
To Scrabster
Gills

SHETLAND ISLANDS

SCALE 7 miles to 1 inch
1:443520
miles

0 1 2 4 6 8 10

0 2 4 8 12 16
kilometres

Muckle Flugga
Herma Ness
HERMANESS   Norwick
Loch of Cliff   Lamba Ness
9086   9087
Haroldswick
Baltasound   KEEN OF HAMAR
Unst   Balta

Gloup   ST OLAF'S ruins
Cullivoe   6
Gossa Water   9082
Gutcher   Uyeasound   MUNESS CASTLE (ruins)
968   KNITWEAR
North Sandwick   Uyea   HAAF GRUNEY
Nev of Stuis
LODGE TOWER
Grimister   Camb   Strandburgh Ness
Hascosay   Fetlar
Hillend   Tresta   Funzie
West Sandwick   9081   9088
Yell
Otterswick
Setter   Hamnavoe
Isbister   OLD HAA
Ulsta   Burravoe
9070   Brough   Copister
Housetter
Roer Water
Ronas Hill 1475   Collafirth
RUBBLE PIER
Urafirth   9019   Ollaberry
TANGWICK HAA   9078   Mossbank
Esha Ness   Hillswick   Hamnavoe
HILLSWICK CRAFTS   17   Sullom   Graven
ESHA NESS DRONGS   9076   LUNNA KIRK
Mangaster   Trondavoe   Bruray
St Magnus Bay   Brae   Housay
968   Out Skerries
10
Muckle Roe   Hillside   Vidlin   Brough   Skaw
5   Laxo   BUNZIE HOUSE
Voe   9071   Symbister   Whalsay
Swarbacks Minn   Dury Voe   HANSEATIC BOOTH   Huxter
Papa Stour   Mid Setter   Vementry   TWEED & KNITWEAR   BROCH OF HUXTER
MINN GUNS   Dury
SEA CAVES   SHEEPSKIN RUGS   9075
Sandness   971   9071   Skellister
Aith   18
SILVERCRAFT
Mainland   Bixter   Weisdale   Girlsta
17   Tresta
Wats Ness   12   Effirth   STANYDALE TEMPLE   Hawks Ness
JEWELLERY   9071   Whiteness   TINGWALL AGRICULTURAL MUS.
Walls   Garderhouse   Heogan
Vaila   Culswick   Veensgarth   Bressay
SHEEPSKINS   9074   Hoversta   Isle of Noss
The Deeps   LERWICK   SHETLAND MUS.
The Kame   Ham   Scalloway   UP-HELLY-A'MUS.
Foula   Hildasay   Kirkabister
South Ness   Oxna   Trondra
Hamnavoe   Easter Quarff   TOWN HALL THEATRE CRAFTS
East Burra
West Burra   To Faeroes & Iceland (Summer only)
Bremirehoull   CUNNINGSBURGH KNITWEAR
South Havra   17   To Norway & Denmark (Summer only)
HOSWICK KNITWEAR   Stove
St Ninians Isle   Mousa   To Stromness & Aberdeen
9122   Levenwick   BROCH OF MOUSA
Scousburgh
Loch of Spiggie   8
Fitful Head   CROFT HOUSE MUSEUM
9070   Sumburgh
Ness of Burgi   Grutness
JARLSHOF   Sumburgh Head

Tourist Information Centres

(S) — Open seasonally

ABERDEEN St. Nicholas House, Broad Street, Aberdeenshire AB9 1DE Tel: (0224) 632727/637353	E2	25
ABERFELDY 8 Dunkeld Street, Perthshire PH15 2DA Tel: (0887) 20276	B1	18
ABERFOYLE (S) Main Street, Perthshire FK8 3TH Tel: (087 72) 352	A3	18
ABINGTON (S) 'Little Chef', A74 Northbound, Lanarkshire Tel: (086 42) 436	E3	13
ABOYNE (S) Ballater Road Car Park, Aberdeenshire Tel: (033 98) 86060	C3	24
ADEN COUNTRY PARK (S) Mintlaw, Aberdeenshire AB4 8LD Tel: (0771) 23037	E3	33
ALFORD (S) Railway Museum, Aberdeenshire Tel: (097 55) 62052	C1	24
ANSTRUTHER (S) Scottish Fisheries Museum, Fife Tel: (0333) 310628	F3	19
ARBROATH Market Place, Angus DD11 1HR Tel: (0241) 72609/76680	F1	19
ARDROSSAN (S) Ferry Terminal Building, Ardrossan Harbour, Ayrshire Tel: (0294) 601063	A2	12
AUCHTERARDER (S) 90 High Street, Perthshire PH3 1BJ Tel: (0764) 63450	C2	18
AVIEMORE Grampian Road, Inverness-shire PH22 1PP Tel: (0479) 810363	E1	23
AYR 39 Sandgate, Ayrshire KA7 1BG Tel: (0292) 284196	B3	12
BALLACHULISH (S) Argyll Tel: (085 52) 296	A4	22
BALLATER (S) Station Square, Aberdeenshire AB3 5RB Tel: (033 97) 55306	B2	24
BALLOCH (S) Balloch Road, Dunbartonshire G83 Tel: (0389) 53533	F4	17
BANCHORY (S) Dee Street Car Park, Aberdeenshire AB3 3YA Tel: (033 02) 2000	D2	25
BANFF (S) Collie Lodge, Banffshire AB4 1AU Tel: (026 12) 2419	D2	33
BETTYHILL (S) Clachan, Sutherland Tel: (064 12) 342	E2	37
BIGGAR (S) 155 High Street, Lanarkshire Tel: (0899) 21066	E3	13
BLAIRGOWRIE 26 Wellmeadow, Perthshire PH10 6AS Tel: (0250) 2960	D1	19
BONAR BRIDGE (S) Sutherland Tel: (086 32) 333	C1	30
BOWMORE (S) Isle of Islay Tel: (049 681) 254	B2	10
BRAEMAR (S) Balnellan Road, Aberdeenshire AB3 5YE Tel: (033 97) 41600	A2	24
BRECHIN (S) St. Ninians Square, Angus Tel: (035 62) 3050	C4	24
BROADFORD (S) Isle of Skye Tel: (047 12) 361/463	D1	21
BRODICK The Pier, Isle of Arran KA27 8AU Tel: (0770) 2140/2401	F3	11
BUCKIE (S) Cluny Square, Banffshire AB5 1HA Tel: (0542) 34853	C2	32
BURNTISLAND 4 Kirkgate, Fife KY3 9HQ Tel: (0592) 872667	D4	19
CALLANDER Ann Caster Square, Perthshire FK17 Tel: (0877) 30342	A3	18
CAMPBELTOWN Argyll PA28 6EF Tel: (0586) 52056	D3	11
CARNOUSTIE The Library, High Street, Angus Tel: (0241) 52258	F1	19
CARRBRIDGE (S) Village Car Park, Inverness-shire Tel: (047 984) 630	E1	23
CASTLEBAY (S) Isle of Barra, Western Isles Tel: (087 14) 336	E3	27
CASTLE DOUGLAS (S) Markethill, Kirkcudbrightshire DG7 2JQ Tel: (0556) 2611	E3	7
COLDSTREAM (S) Henderson Park, Berwickshire TD12 Tel: (0890) 2607	D3	15
CRAIL (S) Museum and Heritage Centre, Marketgate, Fife Tel: (0333) 50869	F3	19
CRIEFF Town Hall, High Street, Perthshire PH7 3HU Tel: (0764) 2578	B2	18
CULLEN (S) 20 Seafield Street, Banffshire AB5 2SH Tel: (0542) 40757	C2	32
CULZEAN CASTLE (S) Ayrshire Tel: (06556) 293	A4	12
CUMNOCK Glasnock Street, Ayrshire Tel: (0290) 23058	C4	12
CUPAR (S) Fluthers Car Park, Fife Tel: (0334) 55555	E2	19
DALBEATTIE (S) Town Hall, Kirkcudbrightshire DG5 Tel: (0556) 610117	E3	7
DALKEITH The Library, White Hart Street, Midlothian EH22 1AE Tel: (031) 663 2083	A1	14
DAVIOT WOOD (S) A9 Nr. Inverness, Inverness-shire Tel: (046 385) 203	D4	31
DORNOCH The Square, Sutherland IV25 3SD Tel: (0862) 810400	D1	31
DUFFTOWN (S) The Square, Banffshire AB5 4AD Tel: (0340) 20501	B3	32
DUMFRIES (S) Whitesands, Dumfries-shire DG1 2SB Tel: (0387) 53862	F2	7
DUNBAR Town House, High Street, East Lothian EH42 Tel: (0368) 63353	F4	19
DUNBLANE (S) Stirling Road, Stirlingshire FK15 Tel: (0786) 824428	B3	18
DUNDEE 4 City Square DD1 3BA Tel: (0382) 27723	E2	19
DUNFERMLINE (S) Glen Bridge Car Park, Fife Tel: (0383) 720999	C4	18
DUNKELD (S) The Cross, Perthshire PH8 0AN Tel: (035 02) 688	C1	18
DUNOON 7 Alexandra Parade, Argyll PA23 8AB Tel: (0369) 3785	A1	12
DURNESS (S) Sango, Sutherland Tel: (097 181) 259	D1	37
EDINBURGH Waverley Market, Princes Street EH2 2QP Tel: (031) 557 1700	F1	13
EDINBURGH Scottish Travel Centre, 14 South St. Andrew Street EH2 2AZ Tel: (031) 557 5522	F1	13
EDINBURGH AIRPORT Tel: (031) 333 2167	F1	13
ELGIN 17 High Street, Moray IV30 1EG Tel: (0343) 543388/542666	B2	32
ELLON (S) Market Street Car Park, Aberdeenshire Tel: (0358) 20730	E4	33
EYEMOUTH (S) Auld Kirk, Berwickshire TD14 Tel: (08907) 50678	D2	15
FALKIRK The Steeple, High Street, Stirlingshire FK1 1EY Tel: (0324) 20244	B4	18
FALKIRK (S) The Mariner Centre, Glasgow Road, Camelon FK1 4HJ Tel: (0324) 611098	B4	18
FOCHABERS (S) Public Institute, High Street, Moray IV32 7EP Tel: (0343) 820770	B3	32
FORFAR (S) The Library, West High Street, Angus DD8 1BA Tel: (0307) 67876	C4	24
FORRES (S) Falconer Museum, Tolbooth Street, Moray IV36 0PH Tel: (0309) 72938	E3	31
FORT AUGUSTUS (S) Car Park, Inverness-shire Tel: (0320) 6367	C1	22
FORTH ROAD BRIDGE (S) By North Queensferry, Fife Tel: (0383) 417759	C4	18
FORT WILLIAM Cameron Square, Inverness-shire PH33 6AJ Tel: (0397) 3781	B3	22
FRASERBURGH (S) Saltoun Square, Aberdeenshire AB4 5DA Tel: (0346) 28315	E2	33
FYVIE (S) Fyvie Castle, Aberdeenshire Tel: (06516) 597	D3	33
GAIRLOCH Achtercairn, Ross-shire IV21 2DN Tel: (0445) 2130	D2	29
GALASHIELS (S) Bank Street, Selkirkshire Tel: (0896) 55551	B3	14
GATEHOUSE OF FLEET (S) Car Park, Kirkcudbrightshire Tel: (055 74) 212	D3	7
GIRVAN (S) Bridge Street, Ayrshire Tel: (0465) 4950	B1	6
GLASGOW 35 St. Vincent Place G1 2ER Tel: (041) 227 4880	C1	12
GLASGOW AIRPORT Inchinnan Road, Paisley, Renfrewshire Tel: (041) 848 4440	B1	12
GLENROTHES Glenrothes House, North Street, Fife KY7 5PB Tel: (0592) 756684	D3	19
GOUROCK (S) The Kiosk, Pierhead, Renfrewshire Tel: (0475) 39467	E4	17
GRANTOWN-ON-SPEY 54 High Street, Morayshire Tel: (0479) 2773	E4	31
GREENOCK Municipal Buildings, 23 Clyde Square, Dumfries-shire PA15 1NB Tel: (0475) 24400	B1	12
GRETNA (S) Annan Road, Dumfries-shire CA6 5HQ Tel: (0461) 37834	B2	8
HAMILTON Roadchef Service Area, M74 Northbound, Nr. Hamilton, Lanarkshire Tel: (0698) 285590	D2	13
HAWICK (S) Common Haugh Car Park, Roxburghshire TD9 Tel: (0450) 72547	B4	14
HELENSBURGH (S) The Clock Tower, Dunbartonshire G84 Tel: (0436) 72642	E4	17
HELMSDALE (S) Couper Park, Sutherland Tel: (043 12) 640	A4	38
HUNTLY (S) 7a The Square, Aberdeenshire Tel: (0466) 2255	C3	32

INVERARAY (S) Front Street, Argyll   Tel: (0499) 2063   D3 17
INVERNESS 23 Church Street, Inverness-shire IV1 1EZ   Tel: (0463) 234353   D3 31
INVERURIE (S) Town Hall, Market Place, Aberdeenshire   Tel: (0467) 20600   D1 25
JEDBURGH Murray's Green, Roxburghshire TD8 6BE   Tel: (0835) 63435/63688   C3 14
JOHN O'GROATS (S) Country Road, Caithness   Tel: (095 581) 373   C1 38
KEITH (S) Church Road, Banffshire AB5 3BR   Tel: (054 22) 2634   B3 32
KELSO (S) Turret House, Roxburghshire TD5 7AX   Tel: (0573) 23464   C3 14
KILLIN (S) Main Street, Perthshire FK21 8UH   Tel: (056 72) 254   A2 18
KILMARNOCK 62 Bank Street, Ayrshire KA1 1ER   Tel: (0563) 39090   B3 12
KINCARDINE BRIDGE (S) Pine 'n' Oak, Kincardine Bridge Road, Stirlingshire   Tel: (032 483) 422   C4 18
KINGUSSIE (S) King Street, Inverness-shire   Tel: (0540) 661297   D2 23
KINROSS (S) Kinross Service Area, M90, Kinross-shire KY13 7BA   Tel: (0577) 63680   C3 18
KIRKCALDY Esplanade, Fife KY1   Tel: (0592) 267775   D3 19
KIRKCUDBRIGHT (S) Harbour Square, Kirkcudbrightshire DG6 4HY   Tel: (0557) 30494   E3 7
KIRKWALL 6 Broad Street, Orkney Islands KW15 1NX   Tel: (0856) 2856   B3 39
KIRRIEMUIR (S) Bank Street, Angus   Tel: (0575) 74097   B4 24
KYLE OF LOCHALSH (S) Car Park, Inverness-shire   Tel: (0599) 4276   D4 29
LANARK Horsemarket, Ladyacre Road, Lanarkshire ML11 7LQ   Tel: (0555) 61661   D2 13
LANGHOLM (S) High Street, Dumfries-shire DG13   Tel: (03873) 80976   B2 8
LARGS Promenade, Ayrshire KA30 8BQ   Tel: (0475) 673765   A2 12
LERWICK The Market Cross, Shetland Islands ZE1 0LU   Tel: (0595) 3434   C3 40
LEVEN South Street, Fife KY8 4PF   Tel: (0333) 29464   E3 19
LINLITHGOW Burgh Halls, The Cross, West Lothian EH49 7AH   Tel: (0506) 844600   C4 18
LOCHBOISDALE (S) Isle of South Uist and Benbecula, Western Isles   Tel: (087 84) 286   D2 27
LOCHCARRON (S) Main Street, Ross-shire   Tel: (05202) 241   E4 29
LOCHGILPHEAD (S) Lochnell Street, Argyll   Tel: (0546) 2344   C4 16
LOCHINVER (S) Main Street, Sutherland   Tel: (057 14) 330   B3 36
LOCHMADDY (S) Isle of North Uist, Western Isles   Tel: (087 63) 321   B2 26
LOCHRANZA (S) Isle of Arran KA27 8HL   Tel: (0770) 83 320   E2 11
MALLAIG (S) Inverness-shire   Tel: (0687) 2170   D2 21
MAUCHLINE National Burns Memorial Tower, Kilmarnock Road, Ayrshire   Tel: (0290) 51916   C3 12
MELROSE (S) Priorwood Gardens, Nr. Abbey, Roxburghshire TD6   Tel: (089 682) 2555   B3 14
MILLPORT (S) Stuart Street, Isle of Cumbrae   Tel: (0475) 530753   A2 12
MILTON (S) By Dumbarton, Dunbartonshire   Tel: (0389) 42306   B1 12
MOFFAT (S) Church Gate, Dumfries-shire DG10 9EG   Tel: (0683) 20620   E4 13
MONTROSE The Library, High Street, Angus   Tel: (0674) 72000   D4 25
MOTHERWELL (S) Motherwell Library, Hamilton Road, Lanarkshire   Tel: (0698) 51311   D2 13
MUSSELBURGH Old Craighall, Granada Service Area (A1), East Lothian   Tel: (031) 653 6172   A1 14
MUSSELBURGH (S) Brunton Hall, East Lothian EH21 6AE   Tel: (031) 665 6597   A1 14
NAIRN (S) 62 King Street, Morayshire   Tel: (0667) 52753   E3 31
NEWTON STEWART (S) Dashwood Square, Wigtownshire DG8 6DQ   Tel: (0671) 2431   C3 6
NORTH BERWICK Quality Street, East Lothian EH39 4HJ   Tel: (0620) 2197   E4 19
NORTH KESSOCK Ross-shire IV1 1XB   Tel: (046 373) 505   D3 31
OBAN Argyll Square, Argyll PA34 4AN   Tel: (0631) 63122   C2 16
PAISLEY Town Hall, Abbey Close, Refrewshire PA11 1JS   Tel: (041) 889 0711   B1 12
PEEBLES (S) Chambers Institute, High Street, Peebleshire EH45 8AG   Tel: (0721) 20138   F3 13
PENCRAIG (S) A1, East Linton, East Lothian   Tel: (0620) 860063   F4 19
PENICUIK The Library, 3 Bellman's Road, Midlothian EH26 0AB   Tel: (0968) 72340   F2 13
PERTH 45 High Street, Perthshire PH1 5TJ   Tel: (0738) 38353   C2 18
PERTH (S) Caithness Glass Car Park, A9 Western City By-Pass, Perthshire PH1 3TZ   C2 18
PETERHEAD (S) 54 Broad Street, Aberdeenshire   Tel: (0779) 71904   F3 33
PITLOCHRY 22 Atholl Road, Perthshire PH16 5BX   Tel: (0796) 2215/2751   E4 23
PORTREE Meall House, Isle of Skye IV51 9BZ   Tel: (0478) 2137   C3 28
PRESTWICK (S) Boydfield Gardens, Ayrshire   Tel: (0292) 79946   B3 12
PRESTWICK AIRPORT Ayrshire   Tel: (0292) 79822   B3 12
RALIA (S) By Newtonmore, Inverness-shire   Tel: (054 03) 253   D2 23
ROTHESAY The Pier, Isle of Bute PA20 9AQ   Tel: (0700) 2151   F1 11
ST. ANDREWS South Street, Fife KY16 9TE   Tel: (0334) 72021   E2 19
SANQUHAR (S) Old Tollbooth, High Street, Dumfries-shire   Tel: (0659) 50185   D4 13
SELKIRK (S) Halliwell's House, Selkirkshire TD7   Tel: (0750) 20054   B3 14
SHIEL BRIDGE (S) Ross-shire   Tel: (0599) 81264   F1 21
SPEAN BRIDGE (S) Inverness-shire   Tel: (039 781) 576   B3 22
STIRLING Dumbarton Road, Stirlingshire FK8 2LQ   Tel: (0786) 75019   B3 18
STIRLING (S) M9/M80 Pirnhall Service Area, Stirlingshire   Tel: (0786) 814111   B4 18
STIRLING (S) Broad Street, Stirlingshire   Tel: (0786) 79901   B3 18
STONEHAVEN (S) Market Square, Kincardineshire AB3   Tel: (0569) 62806   E3 25
STORNOWAY 4 South Beach Street, Isle of Lewis, Western Isles PA87 2XY   Tel: (0851) 3088   D2 35
STRANRAER (S) Port Rodie Car Park, Wigtownshire DG9 0PD   Tel: (0776) 2595   B3 6
STRATHPEFFER (S) The Square, Ross-shire   Tel: (0997) 21415   C3 30
STROMNESS (S) Ferry Terminal Building, The Pier Head, Orkney Islands   Tel: (0856) 850716   A3 39
STRONTIAN (S) Argyll   Tel: (0967) 2131   E4 21
TARBERT (S) Pier Road, Isle of Harris, Western Isles   Tel: (0859) 2011   C4 34
TARBERT (S) Loch Fyne, Argyll   Tel: (088 02) 429   E1 11
TARBET (S) Loch Lomond, Dunbartonshire   Tel: (030 12) 260   F3 17
THURSO (S) Car Park, Riverside, Caithness   Tel: (0847) 62371   B1 38
TILLICOULTRY (S) Clock Mill, Upper Mill Street, Clackmannanshire FK13 6AX   Tel: (0259) 52176   B3 18
TOBERMORY Main Street, Isle of Mull PA75 6NT   Tel: (0688) 2182   D4 21
TOMINTOUL (S) The Square, Banffshire AB3 9ET   Tel: (080 74) 285   A1 24
TROON (S) Municipal Buildings, South Beach, Ayrshire   Tel: (0292) 317696   B3 12
TYNDRUM (S) Inverey Hotel Car Park, Perthshire FK20 8RY   Tel: (083 84) 246   F2 17
ULLAPOOL (S) Ross-shire   Tel: (0854) 2135   F1 28
WICK Whitechapel Road, off High Street, Caithness KW1 4EA   Tel: (0955) 2596   C2 38

Places of Interest

🏰 Castles

Aberdour Castle	D4	19
Ardrossan Castle (ruins)	A2	12
Ardvreck Castle (ruins)	C3	36
Ayton Castle	D2	15
Balfour Castle	B3	39
Balgonie Castle	D3	19
Ballone Castle (ruins)	E1	31
Balvenie Castle (ruins)	B3	32
Blair Castle	E3	23
Borthwick Castle	A2	14
Borve Castle (ruins)	C3	26
Bothwell Castle	C2	12
Braemar Castle	A2	24
Brodick Castle NTS	F3	11
Burleigh Castle (ruins)	C3	18
Caerlaverock Castle (ruins)	F3	7
Cardoness Castle (ruins)	D3	7
Carleton Castle (ruins)	B1	6
Carnasserie Castle (ruins)	C3	16
Carsluith Castle (ruins)	D3	7

Drochil Castle (ruins)	F2	13
Drum Castle NTS	D2	25
Drumlanrig Castle	E1	7
Druminnor Castle	C4	32
Dryhope Tower	A3	14
Duart Castle	C1	16
Duffus Castle (ruins)	A2	32
Dumbarton Castle	B1	12
Dundonald Castle (ruins)	B3	12
Dunnottar Castle (ruins)	E3	25
Dunrobin Castle	E1	31
Dunsgiath Castle (ruins)	D1	21
Dunskey Castle (ruins)	A3	6
Dunstaffnage Castle (ruins)	C1	16
Dunvegan Castle	B3	28
Earlshall Castle	E2	19
Eden Castle (ruins)	D3	33
Edinburgh Castle	F1	13
Edzell Castle (ruins)	C3	24
Eglington Castle	B2	12
Eilean Donan Castle	E4	29
Elcho Castle	D2	19

Tantallon Castle

Lochindorb Castle (ruins)	E4	31
Lochmaben Castle (ruins)	A2	8
Lochnaw Castle (external views only)	A3	6
Lochranza Castle (by appt., ruins)	E2	11
Maclellan's Castle (ruins)	E3	7
Minard Castle	D3	17
Morton Castle (ruins)	F1	7
Muchalls Castle	E2	25
Muness Castle (ruins)	C1	40
Neidpath Castle	F3	13
Newark Castle, Broadmeadows	B3	14
Newark Castle (ruins), Port Glasgow	B1	12
Niddry Castle (under restoration)	E1	13
Noltland Castle	B1	39
Ormiclate Castle (ruins)	D3	27
Penkill Castle (by appt.)	B1	6
Pitsligo Castle (ruins)	E2	33
Ravenscraig Castle	D3	19
Red Castle (ruins)	D4	25
Rothesay Castle (ruins)	F1	11
Roxburgh Castle (site of)	C3	14
St. Andrews Castle	E2	19
Scalloway Castle	B3	40
Slains Castle (ruins)	F4	33
Stirling Castle	B3	18
Strathaven Castle	D2	13
Strome Castle (ruins)	E4	29
Tantallon Castle (ruins)	F4	19
Thirlestane Castle	B2	14
Threave Castle NTS (ruins)	E3	7
Tioram Castle (ruins)	D3	21
Tolquhon Castle (ruins)	E4	33
Turnberry Castle (ruins)	A4	12
Urquhart Castle (ruins)	C4	30

Eilean Donan Castle

Castle Campbell	C3	18
Castle Fraser NTS	D1	25
Castle Girnigoe (ruins)	C2	38
Castle Lachlan (ruins)	D3	17
Castle Menzies	E4	23
Castle of Old Wick (ruins)	C2	38
Castle Sinclair (ruins)	C2	38
Castle Stalker (by appt.)	D1	17
Castle Sween	C4	16
Cathcart Castle (ruins)	C2	12
Cawdor Castle	E3	31
Claypotts Castle	E2	19
Corgarff Castle (ruins)	B1	24
Craig Castle	C1	24
Craigcaffie Castle (ruins)	B3	6
Craigievar Castle NTS	C1	24
Craigmillar Castle (ruins), Edinburgh	F1	13
Craignethan Castle (ruins)	D3	13
Crathes Castle NTS	D2	25
Crichton Castle (ruins)	B2	14
Cubbie Roo's Castle (ruins)	B2	39
Culzean Castle NTS	A4	12
Dean Castle	B3	12
Dirleton Castle (ruins)	E4	19
Doune Castle	B3	18

Fast Castle (ruins)	D1	15
Findlater Castle (ruins)	C2	32
Finlarig Castle (ruins)	A1	18
Floors Castle	C3	14
Fyvie Castle NTS	D3	33
Glamis Castle	E1	19
Gylen Castle (ruins)	C2	16
Hailes Castle (ruins)	C1	14
Hermitage Castle	C1	8
Hoddom Castle (ruins)	A2	8
Hollows Tower	B2	8
Hume Castle	C3	14
Huntingtower Castle	C2	18
Huntly Castle (ruins)	C3	32
Inveraray Castle	D3	17
Kellie Castle NTS	E3	19
Kilchurn Castle	E2	17
Kildrummy Castle (ruins)	C1	24
Kindrochit Castle (ruins)	A2	24
Kisimuil Castle	E3	27
Knock Castle (ruins), Ballater	B2	22
Knock Castle, Skye	E1	21
Lauriston Castle	D4	19
Loch Doon Castle	D1	7
Loch Leven Castle (ruins)	C3	18

🏛 Historic Houses

Abbotsford House	B3	14
Abertarff House	D3	31
Arched House NTS (Carlyle's Birthplace)	A2	8
Ardchattan Priory	D1	17
Bachelors' Club NTS	B3	12
Bachuil (by appt.)	C1	16
Blairquhan Castle	B4	12
Bowhill	B3	14
Brodie Castle NTS	E3	31
Broughton House	E3	7
Buckie House (external views only)	F3	19
Burns' House	F2	7
Carrick House	B2	39
Castle of Park	B3	6
Castle Stuart	D3	31
Culross Palace	C4	18
Dalmeny House	D4	19
Duff House	D2	33
Edinburgh: Historic Houses The Georgian House NTS Gladstone's Land NTS	F1	13

No. 7 Charlotte Square
  NTS
Palace of Holyroodhouse
  (restricted opening)

Falkland Palace NTS	D3	19
Fasque	D3	25
Finlaystone House	B1	12
Glasgow: Historic Houses	C1	12
Hutchesons' Hall NTS		
Provand's Lordship		
The Tenement House		
NTS		
Gosford House	E4	19
Greenknowe Tower	C2	14
Haddo House NTS	E4	33
Hill House, The NTS	E4	17
Hill of Tarvit Mansion	E2	19
House NTS		
Holland House	C1	39
Hopetoun House	C4	18
House of the Binns NTS	C4	18
House of Dun NTS	D4	25
Hugh Miller's Cottage NTS	D2	31
Hunterston House	A2	12
Kinneil House	C4	18
Leith Hall NTS	C4	32
Lennoxlove House	B1	14
Linlithgow Palace	E1	13
Loudoun Hall	B3	12
(restricted opening)		
Manderston	D2	15
Maxwelton House	E1	7
Mellerstain House	C3	14
Melsetter House	A4	39
Michael Bruce's Cottage	D3	19
Pinkie House	A1	14
Pollok House	C2	12
Provan Hall NTS	C1	12
Provost Skene's House	E1	25
Rammerscales	F2	7
Scone Palace	C2	18
Scotstarvit Tower (ruins)	E3	19
Smailholm Tower	C3	14
Souter Johnnie's Cottage	A4	12
NTS		
Stevenson House	B1	14
Tangwick Haa	B2	40
Torosay Castle	C1	16
Torwoodlee House	B3	14
(by appt.)		
Town House NTS	C4	18
Traquair House	A3	14
Vaila Hall	B3	40
Weaver's Cottage NTS	B1	12
Winton House	B1	14

✠ Cathedrals, Abbeys, Churches

Aberlady Church	E4	19
Alloway Kirk	B4	12
Arbroath Abbey (ruins)	F1	19
Arbuthnott Church	D3	25
Auchinleck Church	C3	12
Auld Kirk	B3	12
Balmerino Abbey (ruins)	E2	19
Beauly Priory (ruins)	C3	30
Birnie Church	A3	32
Bowmore Round Church	C2	10
Brechin Cathedral	C4	24
Brechin Round Tower	C4	24
Cambuskenneth Abbey	C3	18
(ruins)		
Canisbay Church	C1	38
Carfin Grotto	D2	13
Castle Semple Collegiate	B2	12
Church		
Chapel Finian (ruins)	C3	6
Church of St. Moluag	E1	35
Church of St. Monan	E3	19
Cille Bharra Chapel (ruins)	E3	27

Iona Abbey

Coldingham Priory (ruins)	D1	15
Collegiate Church of	A1	14
St. Nicholas		
Crathie Church	B2	24
Croick Church	C1	30
Crosskirk Medieval Church	B2	39
(ruins)		
Crossraguel Abbey (ruins)	A4	12
Cruggleton Church	D4	7
Dalmeny Kirk	F1	13
Deer Abbey (ruins)	E3	33
Deskford Church (ruins)	C2	32
Dornoch Cathedral	D1	31
Dryburgh Abbey (ruins)	C3	14
Dunblane Cathedral	B3	18
Dundrennan Abbey (ruins)	E3	7
Dunfermline Abbey	C4	18
Dunglass Collegiate Church	C1	14
(ruins)		
Dunkeld Cathedral	C1	18
Durness Old Church (ruins)	D1	37
Edinburgh: Cathedrals	F1	13
St. Giles' Cathedral		
St. Mary's Cathedral		
(Episc.)		
St. Mary's Cathedral		
(R.C.)		
Edrom Norman Arch	D2	15
Elgin Cathedral (ruins)	A2	32
Eynhallow Church (ruins)	A2	39
Fearn Abbey	D2	31
Fogo Church	C2	14
Fort Augustus Abbey	C1	22
Fortrose Cathedral (ruins)	D3	31
Fyvie Church	D3	33
Gifford Church	B1	14
Glasgow Cathedral	C1	12
Glenluce Abbey (ruins)	B3	6
Greenlaw Church	C2	14
Inchcolm Abbey	D4	19
Inchkenneth Chapel (ruins)	A1	16
Inchmahome Priory (ruins)	A3	18
Inishail Chapel	E2	17
Iona Abbey	A2	16
Italian Church	B3	39
Jedburgh Abbey (ruins)	C4	14
Kelso Abbey	C3	14
Kilkenneth Chapel (ruins)	A1	20
Kilmory Knap Chapel	D1	11
(ruins)		

Kinkell Church (ruins)	D1	25
Kinneff Old Church	D3	25
Kippen Church	A3	18
Kirkapol Chapel (ruins)	A1	20
Lady Kirk	D2	15
Leuchars Norman Church	E2	19
Lincluden Collegiate Church	F2	7
(ruins)		
Lindroes Abbey (ruins)	D2	19
Lunna Kirk	C2	40
Marnoch Old Church	C3	32
Maybole Collegiate Church	B4	12
Melrose Abbey (ruins)	B3	14
Muthill Church and Tower	B2	18
(ruins)		
Old South Uist Church of	D3	27
Scotland		
Ophir Round Church (ruins)	A3	39
Pierowall Medieval Church	B1	39
Pluscarden Abbey	F3	31
Queensberry Aisle	F1	7
Restenneth Priory	C4	24
Rosslyn Chapel	A1	14
Saddell Abbey (ruins)	E3	11

Kelso Abbey

St. Andrew's Cathedral, Inverness	D3	31
St. Andrews Cathedral, St. Andrews	E2	19
St. Bean's Church	C2	18
St. Blane's Chapel	F2	11
St. Bride's Church	D3	13
St. Bridget's Church	F1	13
St. Clement's Church	A1	26
St. Columba's Chapel	E2	35
St. Cormac's Chapel	D1	11
St. Duthus' Chapel (ruins)	D2	31
St. Duthus' Collegiate Church	D2	31
St. John's Chapel (ruins)	D2	33
St. Magnus Cathedral	B3	39
St. Magnus Church	B2	39
St. Mahew's Chapel	F4	17
St. Mary's Chapel, Wyre	B2	39
St. Mary's Chapel (ruins), Bridge of Forss	A1	38
St. Mary's Chapel (ruins), Rothesay	F1	11
St. Mary's Church, Auchindoir	C1	24
St. Mary's Church, Haddington	B1	14
St. Mary's Church, Pitcairn	E4	22
St. Michael's Parish Church	E1	13
St. Ninian's Chapel, Tynet	B2	32
St. Ninian's Chapel (ruins), Isle of Whithorn	D4	7
St. Ninian's Isle Chapel	B2	40
St. Olaf's Church (ruins)	C1	40
St. Peter's Church	B1	38
St. Peter's Episcopal Church	D2	35
St. Tredwell's Chapel	B1	39
Seton Collegiate Church	B1	14
Sweetheart Abbey (ruins)	F3	7
Symington Church	B3	12
Torphichen Church	E1	13
Tullibardine Chapel	B2	18
Whithorn Priory (ruins)	D4	7
Yarrow Kirk	A3	14

✿ Gardens/Botanical Gardens

Abercairny Gardens	B2	18
Achamore House Gardens NTS	D2	11
Achnacloich Woodland Garden	D1	17
Achnashellach Lodge Gardens	E3	29
An Cala	C2	16
Arbigland Gardens	F3	7
Ardanaiseig Gardens	D2	17
Ardchattan Priory Gardens	D1	17
Ardencraig Gardens	F1	11
Ardtornish Estate	C1	16
Arduaine Gardens	C3	16
Ardwell House Gardens	B3	6
Armadale Gardens	D2	22
Balcarres	B3	19
Balgonie Castle Wildlife Garden	D3	19
Balmoral Castle Grounds	B2	24
Bargany Gardens	B1	6
Barguillean Gardens	D2	17
Bellahouston Park, Glasgow	C1	12
Bell's Cherrybank Garden	C2	18
Benmore Younger Botanic Garden	E4	17
Branklyn Garden NTS	C2	18
Brechin Castle Garden	C4	24
Brodick Castle Gardens NTS	F3	11
Candacraig Gardens	B1	24
Carradale House Gardens	E3	11
Castle Kennedy Gardens	B3	6

Cluny House Gardens	E4	23
Crarae Glen Garden	D3	17
Crathes Castle Gardens NTS	D2	25
Cruickshank Botanic Garden	E1	25
Culzean Castle Gardens NTS	A4	12
Dalkeith Park	A1	14
Dawyck Botanic Gardens	F3	13
Dochfour Gardens	C4	30
Drummond Castle Gardens	B2	18
Duthie Park and Winter Gardens	E2	25
Edinburgh Royal Botanic Garden	D4	19
Edzell Castle Gardens	C3	24
Finlaystone House Gardens	B1	12
Galloway House Gardens	D4	6
Glasgow Botanic Gardens	C1	12
Glenapp Castle Gardens	B2	6
Glenarn Gardens	E14	17
Glenfeochan House Gardens	D2	17
Glenwhan Gardens	B3	6
Gowranes (by appt.)	D2	19
Greenbank Garden NTS	C2	12
The Hirsel Grounds and Dundock Wood	D3	15
Hunterston House Gardens	A2	12
Innes House Gardens	B2	32
Inveresk Lodge Garden NTS	A1	14
Inverewe Garden NTS	E1	29
Kailzie Gardens	A3	14
Kelburn Country Centre	A2	12
Kellie Castle Garden NTS	B3	19
Kildrummy Castle Gardens	C1	24
Kilmory Castle Gardens	C4	16
Kilmun Arboretum	E4	17
Kiloran Gardens	A3	16
Kilravock Castle Gardens	D3	31
Kinross House Gardens	C3	18
Kyle House Garden	D4	29
Langwell Gardens and Nursery	B2	38
Leckmelm Shrubbery and Arboretum	A1	30
Leith Hall Garden NTS	C4	32
Lews Castle Gardens	D2	35

Torosay Castle Gardens

Lochalsh Woodland Garden NTS	D4	29
Logan Botanic Garden	B4	6
Malleny House Garden	F1	13
Maxwelton House Gardens	E1	7
Megginch Castle Gardens	D2	19
Mertoun Gardens	C3	14
Monymusk Walled Garden	D1	25
Old Semail Herb Garden	B1	24
Pitmedden Garden NTS	E4	33
Pitmuies Garden	F1	19
Priorwood Garden NTS	B3	14
St. Andrews Botanic Gardens	E2	19
St. Mary's Pleasance	B1	14
Scotherbs	D2	19
Scottish White Heather Farm	A1	12
Strone Gardens	E3	17
Suntrap	F1	13
Threave Garden NTS	E3	7
Torosay Castle Gardens	C1	16
Treshnish	A1	16

🏛 Museums/Art Galleries

Aberdeen Art Gallery	E2	25
Aberdeen Maritime Museum (Provost Ross's House NTS)	E2	25
Allan Ramsay Library	D4	13

Glasgow Botanic Gardens

Highland Croft in The Skye Museum of Island Life

Alyth Folk Museum | B4 | 24
Andrew Carnegie Birthplace Museum | C4 | 18
Angus Folk Museum NTS | E1 | 19
Appin Wildlife Museum | D1 | 17
Arbroath Art Gallery | F1 | 19
Arbroath Museum (Signal Tower) | F1 | 19
Arbuthnot Museum and Art Gallery | F3 | 33
Argyll & Southern Highlanders Museum | B3 | 18
Atholl Countryside Collection | E3 | 23
Auchindrain Open Air Museum of Country Life | D3 | 17
Baird Institute Museum | C3 | 12
Banchory Museum | D2 | 25
Banff Museum | D2 | 33
Barony Chambers Museum and Auld Kirk Museum | C1 | 12
Barrack Street Museum | D2 | 19
Biggar Gasworks Museum | E3 | 13
Black House Museum | D1 | 35
Black Watch Regimental Museum | C2 | 18
Bo'ness and Kinneil Railway Centre | C4 | 18
Border Country Life Museum | B2 | 14
Borreraig Piping Centre | A3 | 28
Boswell Museum (by appt.) | C3 | 12
Brander Museum | C3 | 32
Brechin Museum | C4 | 24
Broughty Castle Museum | E2 | 19
Buckie Maritime Museum | B2 | 32
Burghead Museum | F2 | 31
Burns' Cottage and Museum | B4 | 12
Burns' House Museum | C3 | 12
Burns' Museum | B3 | 12
Burntisland Museum | D4 | 19
Burrell Collection | C2 | 12
Bute Museum | F1 | 11
Cameronians (Scottish Rifles) Regimental Museum | D2 | 13
Campbeltown Museum | D3 | 11
Castle Jail Museum | C3 | 14
Clan Donald Centre—Museum of The Isles | D2 | 21
Clan Donnachaidh Museum | E3 | 23
Clan Gunn Museum | B3 | 38
Clan Macpherson Museum | D2 | 23
Clydebank District Museum | B1 | 12
Colbost Folk Museum | A3 | 28
Corrigall Farm Museum | A2 | 39
Craigcleuch Scottish Explorers Museum | B2 | 8

Craigston Museum | E3 | 27
Crail Museum & Heritage Centre | F3 | 19
Creetown Gem Rock Museum | D3 | 7
Crofter's House Museum | C4 | 28
Cumbernauld and Kilsyth District Museum | B4 | 18
David Livingstone Centre | C2 | 12
Dean Castle Museum | B3 | 12
Dick Institute Museum and Art Gallery | B3 | 12
Dingwall Town House | C3 | 30
Dolls' Museum | C3 | 30
Doune Motor Museum | A3 | 18
Dufftown Museum | B4 | 32
Dumfries Museum | F2 | 7
Dunblane Cathedral Museum | B3 | 18
Dunfermline District Museum and The Small Gallery | C4 | 18
Easdale Island Folk Museum | C2 | 16
Edinburgh: Museums/Art Galleries | F1 | 13
  Braidwood and Rushbrook Museum (by appt.)
  City Art Centre
  Edinburgh Museum
  Fruit Market Gallery
  Huntly House
  John Knox House Museum
  Lady Stair's House
  Museum of Childhood
  Museum of Communication
  National Gallery of Scotland
  Royal Museum of Scotland
  Scottish Agricultural Museum
  Scottish National Gallery of Modern Art
  Scottish National Portrait Gallery
  Scottish United Services Museum
Elgin Museum | A2 | 32
Eochdar Cottage Museum | C3 | 26
Eyemouth Museum | D1 | 15
Falconer Museum | E3 | 31
Falkirk Museum | B4 | 18
Fife Folk Museum | E3 | 19
Fochabers Folk Museum | B2 | 32
Gairloch Heritage Museum | D2 | 29
Galloway Deer Museum | D2 | 7
Gladstone Court Museum | E3 | 13
Glasgow: Museums/Art Galleries | C1 | 12
  Charles Rennie Mackintosh Society
  Collins Gallery
  Glasgow Art Gallery and Museum
  Haggs Castle Museum
  Hunterian Art Gallery
  Hunterian Museum
  Museum of Transport
  People's Palace Museum
  Rutherglen Museum
  Springburn Museum and Exhibition Centre
Glasgow Vennel Conservation Area | B3 | 12
Glencoe & North Lorn Folk Museum | A4 | 22
Glenesk Folk Museum | C3 | 24
Glenluce Motor Museum | B3 | 6
Gordon Highlanders Regimental Museum | E2 | 25
Grampian Transport Museum | C1 | 24
Grangemouth Museum | C4 | 18

Greenhill Covenanters' House | E3 | 13
Groam House Museum | D3 | 31
Haddington Museum | B1 | 14
Halliwell's House Museum & Art Gallery | B3 | 14
Hamilton District Museum | D2 | 13
Hanseatic Booth | C3 | 40
Harbour Cottage Gallery | E3 | 7
Hawick Museum & The Scott Art Gallery | B4 | 14
Heatherbank Museum of Social Work | C1 | 12
Henry Duncan Cottage Museum | A2 | 8
Highland Discovery Centre | D2 | 17
Highland Folk Museum | D2 | 23
Highland Motor Heritage Centre | C1 | 18
Highland Tryst Museum | B2 | 18
Hirsel Homestead Museum | D3 | 15
Inverkeithing Museum | F1 | 13
Inverness Museum & Art Gallery | D3 | 31
Inverurie Museum | D1 | 25
Isle of Arran Heritage Museum | F3 | 11
James Dun's House | E2 | 25
Jim Clark Memorial Trophy Room | C2 | 14
John Buchan Centre | E3 | 13
John Hastie Museum | C2 | 12
John McDouall Stuart Museum | D3 | 19
Kelso Museum | C3 | 14
Kinneil Museum and Roman Fortlet | C4 | 18
Kinross Museum | C3 | 18
Kirbuster Farm Museum | A2 | 25
Kirkcaldy Museum & Art Gallery | D3 | 19
Kirkwall, Tankerness House Museum | B3 | 39
Ladycroft Farm Museum | B3 | 32
Largs Museum | A2 | 12
Lhaidhay Croft Museum | B3 | 38
Lillie Art Gallery | C1 | 12
Lochbroom Highland Museum | A1 | 30
McEwan Gallery | B2 | 24
McLean Museum | B1 | 12
McManus Galleries | D2 | 19
Mary Queen of Scots' House | C3 | 14
Meigle Museum | D1 | 19
Melrose Motor Museum | B3 | 14
Montrose Museum | D4 | 25
Moray Motor Museum | A2 | 32
Mull & Iona Folklore Museum | D4 | 20
Murison Burns Collection | C4 | 18
Museum of Farming Life NTS | E4 | 33
Museum of Flight | E4 | 19
Museum of Islay | B2 | 10
Museum of Scottish Tartans | B2 | 18
Museum of The Cumbraes | A2 | 12
Museum of the Scottish Lead Mining Industry | D4 | 13
Myreton Motor Museum | E4 | 19
Nairn Fishertown Museum | E3 | 31
Newton Stuart Museum | C3 | 6
North Ayrshire Museum | A3 | 12
North Berwick Museum | F4 | 19
North East of Scotland Agricultural Heritage Centre | E3 | 33
Norwood Museum | B3 | 39
Oban Museum | D2 | 17
Old Bridge House Museum | F2 | 7

Old Byre Heritage Centre	C4	20
Old Gala House	B3	14
Old Haa	C2	40
Old Smiddy Museum	B4	39
Orcadia Folk Studio, Stromness	A3	39
Orkney Wireless Museum	B4	39
Paisley Museum and Art Gallery	B1	12
Perth Art Gallery and Museum	C2	18
Pier Arts Centre, Stromness	A3	39
Pittencrieff House Museum	C4	18
Queen's Own Highlanders Museum	D3	31
Queensferry Museum	C4	18
'Remains to be Seen'	E4	33
Robert Burns Centre	F2	7
Robert Smail's Printing Works NTS	A3	14
Robertson Museum	A2	12
St. Vigeans Museum	F1	19
Sanquhar Museum (by appt.)	D4	13
Scalloway Museum	B3	40
Scottish Fisheries Museum	E3	19
Scottish Horse Museum	C1	18
Scottish Industrial Railway Centre	B4	12
Scottish Maritime Museum	B3	12
Scottish Mining Museum, Newtongrange	A1	14
Scottish Mining Museum, Prestongrange	B1	14
Scottish Museum of Woollen Textiles	A3	14
Shambellie House Museum of Costume	F3	7
Shawbost Folk Museum	D1	35
Shetland Croft House Museum	B4	40
Shetland Museum	C3	40
Skerry Vore Museum	A1	20
Skye Museum of Island Life	B2	28
Smith Art Gallery and Museum	B3	18
Stewartry Museum	E3	7
Stonehaven Tolbooth Museum	E3	25
Stornoway Museum	D2	35
Strathallan Aircraft Museum	B2	18
Strathnaver Museum	E2	37
Stromness Museum	A3	39
Summerlee Heritage Trust	D1	13
Tain and District Museum	D1	31
Tam O'Shanter Museum	B3	12
Thomas Muir Museum	C1	12
Thurso Folk Museum	B1	38
Tingwell Agricultural Museum	C3	40
Tobias Smollett Collection	F4	17
Tomintoul Museum	A1	24
Tweeddale Museum	A3	14
Up-Helly-A' Museum	C3	40
Viewfield Museum	E3	31
West Highland Museum	B3	22
Whithorn Museum	D4	7
Wick Heritage Centre	C2	38
Wigtown District Museum	B3	6
William Lamb Memorial Studio	D4	25
Woodside Studio Gallery	E3	7

Ancient Monuments, Monuments

Aberlemno Sculptured Stones	C4	24
Abernethy Round Tower	D2	19
Achavanich Standing Stones	B3	38
Alexander III Monument	D4	19
Annie Jane Monument	E3	27
Antonine Wall	B4	18
Ardclach Bell Tower	E3	31
Ardestie & Carlungie Earth Houses	F1	19
Ardoch Roman Camp	B3	18
Barochan Cross	B1	12
Barpa Langass	B2	26
Barsalloch Fort	C4	6
Bell Obelisk	B1	12
Bernera Barracks	E1	21
Birrens Roman Fort	A2	8
Bishop's Palace, Kirkwall	B3	39
Black Watch Memorial	B1	18
Bonnie Prince Charlie's Monument	D2	35
Bornish Standing Stone	D3	27
Brandsbutt Stone	D1	25
Broch, Bronze Age House & Iron Age Fort, Clickimin Lerwick	C3	40
Broch of Burrian	C1	39
Broch of Huxter	C3	40
Broch of Mousa	C4	40
Brough of Birsay	A2	39
Brough of Deerness	B3	39
Bruce's Stone NTS, Clatteringshaws Loch	D2	6
Bruce's Stone, Loch Trool	C2	6
Bunzie House	C2	40
Burns Family Tombstone and Cairn	D3	25
Burns' Monument	B4	12
Burnswark Hillfort and Roman Camp	A2	8
Cairn of Get (Garrywhin Chambered Cairn)	C3	38
Cairnpapple Hill	E1	13
Callanish Standing Stones	C2	34
Campbeltown Celtic Cross	D3	11
Captain Scott and Dr. Wilson Fountain	B4	24
Carloway Broch	C2	34
Castlelaw Souterrain	F1	13
Caterthuns, The	C3	24
Clach An Trushal	D1	35
Clach Mhicleoid (Macleod's Stone)	C4	34
Clachtoll Broch	B3	36
Clackmannan Tower	B4	18
Clava Cairns NTS	D3	31
Commando Memorial	B2	22
Corrimony Cairn	B4	30
Coulter Motte	E3	13
Cross Kirk	A2	14
Cullerlie Stone Circle	D2	25
Culloden 1746 NTS	D3	31
Culsh Earthwork	C2	24
Cuween Hill Chambered Tomb	B3	39
Dogton Stone	D3	19
Drumcoltran Tower	E2	7
Drumtroddan Rock Carvings	C4	6
Dun Da Lamh	D2	23
Dun Dornaigil Broch	D2	37
Dunadd Fort	C3	16
Duns Scotus Statue	C2	14
Dunsinane Hillfort	D2	19
Dwarfie Stane	A3	39
Dyce Symbol Stone	E1	25
Eagle Stone	C3	30
Earl Patrick's Palace, Kirkwall	B3	39
Earl's Palace	A2	39
Eassie Sculptured Stone	D1	19
East Aquhorthies Stone Circles	D1	25
Edin's Hall Broch	C2	14
Flodden Monument	B3	14
Flora MacDonald's Birthplace	D3	27
Flora MacDonald Monument	D3	31
Fowlis Wester Sculptured Stones	B2	18
Fort Charlotte, Lerwick	C3	40
Fyrish Monument	C2	30
George Buchanan Obelisk	A4	18
Glenelg Brochs	E1	21
Glenfinnan Monument NTS	F3	21
Grey Cairns of Camster	B2	38
Gurness Broch	B2	39
Highland Mary's Monument	B3	12
Hill o'Many Stanes	B3	38
James Hogg Monument	F4	13

Carloway Broch

Callanish Standing Stones

Ruthwell Cross	A2	8
St. Fillan's Cave	E3	19
St. Orland's Stone	B4	24
St. Serf's Tower (by appt.)	D3	19
Skara Brae	A3	39
Skelmorlie Aisle	A2	12
Smollett Monument	F4	17
Stanydale Temple	B3	40
Standing Stones of Machrie Moor	E3	11
Steinacleit	D1	35
Stones of Stenness	A3	39
Strichen Stone Circle	E3	33
Suenos Stone	E3	31
Tarves Medieval Tomb	E4	33
Tealing Earth House and Dovecote	E1	19
Telford Memorial	B1	8
Tinnis Castle	F3	13
Tomb of Eagles	B4	39
Tomnaverie Stone Circle	C2	24
Torhousekie Stone Circle	C3	6
Trinity Temple	C2	27
Wallace Memorial	B1	12
Wallace Monument	B3	18
Waterloo Monument	C3	14
White Horse, Mormond Hill	E3	33
Wideford Hill Chambered Tomb	B3	39
Wren's Egg Stone Circle	C4	6

 Zoos, Wildlife Parks

Argyll Wildlife Park	C3	17
Blair Drummond Safari Park	B3	18
Cluanie Deer Farm Park	C3	30
Edinburgh Butterfly and Insect World	A1	14
Edinburgh Zoo	F1	13
Fairways Heavy Horse Centre	D2	19
Glasgow Zoo	C2	12
Glengoulandie Deer Park	E4	23
Highland Wildlife Park	E2	23
New Lanark Wildlife Centre	D3	13
Oban Rare Breeds Farm Park	D2	17
Robertson Aquarium	A2	12
Scottish Deer Centre	D2	19
Sea Life Centre, Oban	D1	17

James Thomson Obelisk	C3	14
Jarlshof Broch and Settlement	B4	40
Jarlshof Long Houses	B4	40
John Cobb Memorial	C4	30
Keir Hardie Monument	C3	12
Kempock Stone	E4	17
Kenneth Murray Memorial	D4	37
Kilberry Sculptured Stones	D1	11
Kildalton Crosses	C2	10
Kilmartin Sculptured Stones	C3	16
Kilmory Cairns	E3	11
Kilpheder Wheelhouse	D3	27
Kirkmadrine Stone	B3	6
Knowe of Onston	A3	39
Laggangairn Standing Stones	B2	6
Leyden Obelisk & Tablet	B4	14
Loanhead Stone Circle	D4	33
Loch Nan Uamh Cairn	E3	21
Lodge Tower	C1	40
Lybster Celtic Cross	B3	38
Lyte Plaque	C3	14
McCaig's Tower	C2	16
Macdonald Tower	C2	30
Macpherson Monument	E2	23
Maes Howe	A3	39
Maiden Stone	D4	33
Maison Dieu	C4	24
Marjoribanks Monument	D3	15
Martello Tower	A4	39
Martyrs' Monument	C3	6
Melville Monument	B2	18
Memsie Burial Cairn	E2	33
Merkland Cross	A2	8
Minn Guns	B3	40
Monument Hill	E2	17
Moss Farm-Road Stone Circle	E3	11
Mote of Mark NTS	E3	7
Mote of Urr	E3	7
Murray's Monument	D2	7
Nelson Tower	E3	31
Ness of Burgi	B4	40
Nether Largie Cairns	C3	16
Old Place of Mochrum (Drumwalt Castle)	C3	6
Old Village of Badbea	B4	38
Orchardton Tower	E3	7

Ousdale Broch	A4	38
Peel Ring of Lumphanan	C2	24
Picardy Stone	C4	32
Pobull Fhinn	B2	26
Prestonpans Battle Cairn	B1	14
Quoyness Chambered Tomb	C2	39
Rennibister Earth House	B3	39
Renwick Monument	E1	7
Ring of Brogar	A3	39
Rob Roy's Grave	A2	18
Rob Roy's Statue	D2	25
Robinson Crusoe Statue	E3	19
Roderick Mackenzie Memorial	B1	22
Rosal Clearance Village	E3	37
Rough Castle	B4	18
Ruthven Barracks	E2	23

Red Deer on Ben Alder

Sea Life Centre, St. Andrews	E2	19
Seaworld	B3	12
Skyreburn Aquarium	D3	7
South Bank Farm Park	F3	11
Tropical Butterfly House	C3	18

Bird Sanctuaries/ Nature Reserves

Balranald Nature Reserve	B3	26
Barons Haugh Nature Reserve	D2	13
Beinn Eighe National Nature Reserve	E2	29
Ben Lawyers National Nature Reserve	A1	18
Birsay Moors Nature Reserve	A2	39
Caerlaverock National Nature Reserve	F3	7
Caerlaverock Wildfowl and Wetlands Centre	F3	7
Cairngorms National Nature Reserve	F2	23
Copinsay Nature Reserve	C3	39
Corehouse Nature Reserve	D3	13
Craigellachie National Nature Reserve	E1	23
Creag Meagaidh National Nature Reserve	C2	22
Doune Ponds Nature Reserve	B3	18
Duns Castle Reserve	C2	14
Fetlar	C1	40
Foula	A3	40
Fowlsheugh Seabird Colony	E3	25
Glen Roy National Nature Reserve	B2	22
Glen Tanar Estate	C2	24
Haaf Gruney National Nature Reserve	C1	40
Handa Island Nature Reserve	B2	36
Hermaness National Nature Reserve	C1	40
Hobbister	B3	39
Inverpolly National Nature Reserve	C4	36
Keen of Hamar National Nature Reserve	C1	40
Kylerhea Otter Haven	E1	21
Lindean Reservoir Nature Reserve	B3	14
Loch Druidibeg National Nature Reserve	D2	27
Loch Garten Nature Reserve	F1	23
Loch Leven National Nature Reserve	D3	19
Loch Lomond National Nature Reserve	F4	17
Loch of Lowes Nature Reserve	C1	18
Loch of Spiggie	B4	40
Lochwinnoch Nature Reserve	B2	12
The Loons	A2	39
Marwick Head	A2	39
Montrose Basin Nature Reserve	D4	25
Muir of Dinnet National Nature Reserve	C2	24
North Hill	B1	39
North Hoy	A3	39
Noss National Nature Reserve	C3	40
Noup Cliffs	B2	39
Rhum National Nature Reserve	B2	20

St. Abb's Head National Nature Reserve	D1	15
St. Cyrus National Nature Reserve	D3	25
Sands of Forvie National Nature Reserve	E4	33
Strathy Bog National Nature Reserve	F2	37
Tentsmuir Point National Nature Reserve	E2	19
Threave Wildfowl Refuge NTS	E3	7
Trumland	B2	39
Vane Farm Wildlife Reserve	C3	18
Wood of Cree Nature Reserve	C2	6

Nature Trails, Forest Parks

Abernethy Glen	D2	19
Achray Forest	F3	17
Achriabhach Forest Walk	B3	22
Ae Forest Walks	F1	7
Aigas Nature Trails	C3	30
Allean Forest Walks	E4	23
Arbroath Cliff's Nature Trail	F1	19
Ardentinny to Carrick	E4	17
Ardessie Waterfalls	F1	29
Ardgartan Forest Walks	E3	17
Ardmore Point Nature Trail	C4	20
Aros Park	D4	21
Back o'Bennachie Forest Walks	D4	33
Balmaha Trail	F3	17
Banchory Forest Walks	C3	24
Banff, Whitehills & Aberchirder	D2	33
Beinn Lora Walks	D1	17
Belmont Estate Nature Trail	D1	19
Ben A' An	A3	18
Ben Lomond NTS	F3	17
Ben Vorlich	A2	18
Big Burn Waterfall Walk	F4	37
Birks of Aberfeldy	B1	18
Blackstand Walks	D3	31
Blairadam and Edensmuir Forest Walks	D3	19
Borgie Trails	E2	37
Bowhill Walks	B3	14
Brae Walk	C2	30

Brodick Woodland Walk	F3	11
Brodie Castle Woodland Walk NTS	E1	31
Bull Loch Trail	F1	11
Burg, The	A2	16
Cardrona Walks	A3	14
Carradale Forest	E3	11
Carron Valley Forest	A4	18
Clunes Forest	B2	22
Corehouse Woodland Trails	D3	13
Cornalees Bridge Nature Trail	A1	12
Corrychurrachon	A3	22
Coulmore Wood Walk	C3	30
Craig Phadrig Forest Walk	D3	31
Craighall Den	E3	19
Craigievar Castle Woodland Walk NTS	C1	24
Craigower/Dunmore Trail NTS	E4	23
Craik Forest Trail	A4	14
Crathes Castle Woodland Trails	D2	25
Crieff Nature Trail	B2	18
Cromarty Foreshore Walks	D2	31
Culbokie Loch Walk	C3	30
Culloden Forest Trail	D3	31
Dalkeith Park Nature Trails	A1	14
Dog Falls	B4	30
Dollar Glen Nature Trail NTS	C3	18
Don View	D1	25
Drum Castle Woodland Walk NTS	D2	25
Drumlanrig Castle Walks	E1	7
Drummond Hill Forest Walks	B1	18
Dulsie Bridge Country Walk	E3	31
Dun Na Cuaiche Woodland Walk	E3	17
Dunnikier Park Nature Trail	D3	19
Eas Na Circe	D1	17
Eildon Walk	B3	14
Elgin Town Trail	B2	32
Enterkine Wood	B3	12
Ettrick Bay Trail	F1	11
Falls of Bruar Country Walk	E3	23
Falls of Divach	C4	30
Farigaig Forest Trail	C4	30
Faskally Forest Walks	E4	23

Loch Corulsk

Fearnoch Forest — D2 17
Fionn Loch — E2 29
Five Sisters of Kintail NTS — F1 21
Fleet Forest Trails — D3 7
Flowerdale Falls — D2 29
Fortrose Walks — D3 31
Fountainbleau and Ladypark Reserve Nature Trail — F2 7
Galloway Forest Park — C2 6
Gearcholile Community Wood Trail — C1 30
Glen Affric River Walk — F4 29
Glen Dubh — D1 17
Glen Lednock Circular Walk — B2 18
Glen Ogle Trail — A2 18
Glencoe & Dalness NTS — B4 22
Glendaruel Forest — D4 17
Glengarry Forest Walk — B2 22
Glenloy Forest — B3 22
Glenmore Forest Trails — F1 23
Glentarken Wood Walk — A2 18
Glentress Forest Trails — A3 14
Glenvarragill Walk — C3 28
Goatfell NTS — F3 11
Haddington — B1 14
Hazlehead Nature Tracks — D2 25
Hermitage Forest Woodland Trail — C1 18
Hermitage of Braid, Edinburgh — F1 13
Inchnacardoch Forest Walks — C1 22
Inverliever Forest Walks — D3 17
Jock's Road & Capel Track — B3 24
Jubilee Walks — D2 19
Kilmuir Walk — D3 31
Kilsture Forest Walk — C3 6
Kindrogan Field Centre — F4 23
Kingarth Trail — F2 11
Kinloch Glen & South Side Nature Trails — C2 20
Kinnoull Hill Trails — C2 18
Kirkhill Forest Walks — D2 25
Knapdale Forest Walk — C3 16
Knockan Cliff Nature Trail — C4 36
Kyle of Sutherland Forest Walks — C1 30
Lael Forest Garden Trail — F2 29
Laigh of Moray Forest Walks — A3 32
Lairigmor — B4 22
Lanark Loch and Moor — E3 13
Landmark Woodlands & Trails — E1 23
Larg Hill & Bruntis Trails — C3 6
Leith Hall Nature Trails NTS — C4 32
Letham Glen Nature Trail — E3 19
Linn Park Nature Trail — C2 12
Linn of Tummel Trails NTS — E4 23
Loch Ard Forest Trails — F3 17
Loch Trool Forest Trail — C2 6
Lochalsh Walks, Balmacara — D4 29
Lochan Forest Trail — A4 22
Mains of Eathie Walks — D2 31
Mearns Forest Walks — D3 25
Mill Glen Nature Trail — C3 18
Morangie Forest Walk — D1 31
Mounthigh — E2 31
Muir of Tarradale — C3 30
Munlochy Bay and Ormond Hill Walks — D3 31
Murray Park Nature Trail — C1 24
Ord Hill Walk — D3 31
Paisley Glen — C2 12
Pattack Falls Forest Walk — D2 23
Pencaitland Railway Walk — B1 14
Pitmedden — E4 33
Plantain Loch & Dalbeattie Forest Walks — E3 7

Portsay & Sandend Coastal Walks — C2 32
Pressmennan Forest Trail — C1 14
Provost's Walk — C3 18
Puck's Glen — E4 17
Rannoch Forest Walks — D4 23
Ravenscraig Park Nature Trail — D4 19
Redcastle — C3 30
Reelig Glen Forest Walk — C3 30
Rock Wood Ponds Forest Walk — E2 23
Rogie Walk — C3 30
Ross Hall Park Nature Trails — C2 12
Rothesay Walk, Loch Fad & Loch Ascog Trail — F1 11
Rozelle Park Nature Trail — B4 12
Rumster — B3 38
St. Michael's Forest Walk — D2 31
Sallochy Trail — F3 17
Seafield Walkway — D4 19
Secret Valley Walks — E3 31
Signal Rock Trail — B4 22
Silverburn Estate Trails — E3 19
Slattadale Forest Trail & Tollie Path — D2 29
Solway Mabie Walks — F2 7
South End of Bute Trail — F2 11
Southern Upland Way — A3 6
Southern Upland Way — C1 14
Speymouth Forest Walks — B3 32
Speyside Way — B2 32
Speyside Way — B3 32
Springburn — C1 12
Stome Wood — E4 29
Storr Nature Trail — C3 28
Strathy Point Nature Trail — F1 37
Strathyre Forest Information Centre & Walks — A2 18
Stroan Bridge Forest Trails — C2 6
Strontian Glen Nature Trail — E4 21
Talnotry Forest Trail — D2 7
Thornylee Forest Walks — B3 14
Threave House Trail — E3 7
Tighnabruaich — F1 11
Tomintoul Country Walk — A1 24
Tore School Walk — C3 30
Torrachilty Forest Trail — C3 30
Torridon NTS — E3 29
Tummel Forest Park Walks — E4 23
Ullapool — A1 30
Vane Farm Nature Trail — C3 18
Water of Leith, Edinburgh — F1 13
White Cow Forest Walks — E3 33
Wildering Forest Walks — F3 17
Woodland Centre Walks — C3 14
Wrack Woodland Path — D2 33
Yellowcraigs Nature Trail — E4 19

Country Parks
Aden Country Park — E3 33
Almondell and Calderwood Country Park — E1 13
Balloch Castle Country Park — F4 17
Balmedie Country Park — E1 25
Beecraigs Country Park — E1 13
Bonaly Country Park — F1 13
Brodick Country Park NTS — F3 11
Calderglen Country Park — C2 12
Camperdown and Templeton Woods Country Park — D2 19
Castle Semple Country Park — B2 12
Chatelherault Country Park — D2 13
Clatto Country Park — E1 19
Craigtoun Country Park — E2 19
Crombie Country Park — E1 19
Culzean Country Park NTS — A4 12
Dean Castle Country Park — B3 12

Drumpellier Country Park — D1 13
Eglinton Country Park — B2 12
Forfar Loch Country Park — C4 24
Gartmorn Dam Country Park — B3 18
Gleniffer Braes Country Park — B2 12
Haddo Country Park — E4 33
Haughton House Country Park — C1 24
Hillend Country Park — F1 13
John Muir Country Park — F4 19
Lochore Meadows Country Park — D3 19
Millbuies Country Park — B3 32
Monikie Country Park — E1 19
Mugdock Country Park — A4 18
Muiravonside Country Park — E1 13
Muirshiel Country Park — B1 12
Palacerigg Country Park — D1 13
Polkemmet Country Park — E1 13
Pollok Country Park — C2 12
Strathclyde Country Park — D2 13
Vogrie Country Park — A1 14

Other Tourist Features
Abbey St. Bathans Trout Farm — C2 14
Aberfeldy Distillery — E4 23
Alford Valley Railway — C1 24
Andrew Abrahams Oyster Farm — A3 16
Ardessie Waterfalls — F1 29
Aviemore Centre — E1 23
Balnakeil Craft Village — D1 37
Bannockburn NTS — B4 18
Barrie's Birthplace NTS — B4 24
Baxters of Speyside Visitors Centre — B2 32
Bealach-Na-Ba — D3 29
Bell's Bladnoch Distillery — C3 6
Ben Nevis — B3 22
Birkhill Clay Mine — C4 18
Black House Village (ruins) — C2 34
Black Rock Gorge — C2 30
Blair Atholl Distillery — F4 23
Blowplain Open Farm — D2 7
Boardhouse Mill — A2 39
Boath Doocot NTS — E3 31
Bo'ness and Kinneil Railway — C4 18
Bonawe Iron Furnace — D2 17
Border Collie and Shepherd Centre — E4 13
Braeloine Interpretive Centre — C3 24
Brenish Pottery & Tweeds — B2 34
Bridge o'Dee — E2 25
Bridge of Carr — E1 23
Bullers of Buchan — F4 33

Preston Mill

Ben Nevis

Burghead Well F2 31
Burns' Mausoleum F2 7
Burns' Memorial Tower C3 12
Caithness Glass, Oban D2 17
Caithness Glass, Perth C2 18
Caithness Glass, Wick C2 38
Caledonian Canal C2 22
Cambo Country Park F3 19
Camphill Village Trust E2 25
Cape Wrath C1 36
Cardhu Distillery A3 32
Cassley Waterfall D4 37
Churchill Barriers B3 39
Clan MacAlister Centre D3 11
Click Mill A2 39
Clock Mill Inter Centre B3 18
Clynelish Distillery F4 37
Coldstream Mains Fruit D3 15
  Farm
Coll Pottery E2 35
Corrieshalloch Gorge NTS F2 29
Corryvreckan Whirlpool C3 16
Cove Harbour C1 14
Cragganmore Distillery A4 32
Craigellachie Bridge B3 32
Crail Tolbooth F3 19
Crawford Centre for the E2 19
  Arts
Crieff Visitors Centre B2 18
Crimonmogate Fishery E3 33
Croft-na-Caber Watersports B1 18
  and Activities Centre
Crook of Devon Fish Farm C3 18
Cruachan Pump Storage D2 17
  Power Station
Cunningsburgh Knitwear C4 40
Dalgarven Mill B2 12
Dallas Dhu Distillery E3 31
Dalwhinnie Distillery D2 23
Darnaway Farm Visitor E3 31
  Centre
David Marshall Lodge A3 18
  (Forest Park Visitor
  Centre)
Denny Tank, The B1 12
Devil's Beef Tub E4 13
Dig, The C3 6
Dornoch Craft Centre and D1 31
  Town Jail

Dounreay Nuclear Power A1 38
  Development
  Establishment
Druimgwigwa Ecological C4 20
  Farm and Stud
Drumlanwig Castle Craft E1 7
  Centre
Drummond Fish Farm B2 18
Dunaverty Rock D4 11
Dunbeath Heritage Centre B3 38
Duncansby Head and C1 38
  Stacks
Dunnet Head B1 38
Eas-Coul-Aulin C3 36
Easter Weens Cheese Farm C4 14
Eden Court Theatre C3 30
Edinburgh: Other Tourist F1 13
  Features
  Brass Rubbing Centre
  Canongate Tolbooth
  Gorgie City Farm
  Scotch Whisky Heritage
  Centre
Edinburgh Crystal Works F2 13
Elwick Mill B3 39
Esha Ness Drongs B2 40
Farigaig Forest Centre C4 30
Falls of Glomach NTS E4 29
Falls of Kirkaig B4 36
Falls of Pattack D2 23
Falls of Rogie C3 30
Falls of Shin C1 30
Fettercairn Arch D3 25
Finavon Doocot C4 24
Fingal's Cave A1 16
Fordyce C2 32
Fort George D3 31
Fortingall Yew B1 18
Gisla Woodcraft C3 34
Glen Grant Distillery B3 32
Glenaray Fish Farm D3 17
Glendronach Distillery C3 32
Glenfarclas Distillery A4 32
Glenfiddich Distillery B3 32
Glengarioch Distillery D4 33
Glengoyne Distillery F4 17
Glenkinchie Distillery B1 14
Glenlivet Distillery A4 32
Glenturret Distillery B2 18

Globe Inn F2 7
Gloup, The B3 39
Gondola Cable Car, B3 22
  Aonach Mor
Gravamore Bridge C2 22
Great Glen (Highland C1 22
  Heritage Exhibition)
Great Scots Visitor Centre C3 18
Grey Mare's Tail NTS F4 13
Harness Racing E3 13
Harray Pottery A3 39
Hermitage, The C1 18
Highland Park Distillery, B3 39
  Kirkwall
Hoswick Tweed & Knitwear B2 40
Hydroponicum, The B4 36
Inchgower Distillery C2 32
Inverallochy E2 33
Inveraray Bell Tower C3 17
Inveraray Jail C3 17
Isle of Mull Railway C1 16
James Stewart Tablet A4 22
Jewellery, Walls B3 40
Keith Statue F3 33
Kilt Rock C2 28
Kings Cave E3 11
Kirk Yetholm D3 15
Kirroughtree Visitor Centre D3 7
Kyles of Bute D4 17
Lady Gifford's Well F2 13
Land O' Burns Centre B3 12
Landmark Visitor Centre E1 23
Lerwick, Garrigon Theatre C3 40
Lerwick Town Hall C3 40
Lhaidhay Caithness Craft B1 38
Library and Orkney Room, B3 39
  Kirkwall
Livingston Mill Farm E1 13
Loch Morar E2 21
Loch Ness C1 22
Loch Ness Monster C4 30
  Exhibition
Lochearn Sailing and A2 18
  Watersports Centre
Lochty Private Railway E3 19
  (restricted opening)
Logan Fish Pond B4 6
Login's Well A3 39
Lower City Mills C2 18
Lyness Naval Base A3 39
Maltings Fishery C1 14
Meal and Flour Mill E3 23
Meikleour Beech Hedge D1 19
Mills Observatory E2 19
Moat Park Heritage Centre E3 13
Monarch Deer Farm C3 18
Monktonhill Fruit Farm B3 12
My Lord's Throat D1 25
  (Scenic Drive)
Neptune's Staircase B3 22
New Abbey Corn Mill F3 7
New Lanark Conservation D3 13
  Village
New Lighthouse C1 39
North Berwick Law E4 19
North Glen Gallery E3 7
Oban Distillery D2 17
Old Beacon C1 39
Old Blacksmith's Shop B2 8
Old Man of Stoer B3 36
Old Mill Visitor Centre B4 32
Old Mills A2 32
Ord Distillery C3 30
Orkney Angora C2 39
Orkney Arts Theatre, B3 39
  Kirkwall
Orkney Tweeds C2 39
Orinsay, Crafts D3 35
Palgowan Open Farm C2 6
Papa Stour Sea Caves A3 40
Parallel Roads B2 22

Dinghy Sailing at Largs

Pass of Killiecrankie NTS	E4	23
Pitlochry Power Station Visitor Centre	E4	23
Poosie Nansie's Tavern	B3	12
Preston Mill and Phantassie Doocot NTS	F4	19
Quiraing	C2	28
R.R.S. Discovery	E2	19
Raasay Outdoor Centre	C4	28
Raiders' Road Forest Drive	D2	7
Randolph's Leap	E3	31
Rennie Memorial	F4	19
Rennie's Bridge	C3	14
Rothiemurchus Visitor Centre	E1	23
Royal Lochnagar Distillery	B2	24
Rubble Pier	B2	40

Russell Gurney Weavers	D3	33
St. Columba's Cave	C4	16
St. Columba's Footsteps	D4	11
Sanday Knitwear	C2	39
Sanquhar Post Office	D4	13
Scots Dyke	B2	8
Scottish Craft and Ben Nevis Exhibition	B2	22
Scott's View	C3	14
Sculpture Workshops	C1	24
Selkirk Glass	B3	14
Sheepskin Rugs, Aith	B3	40
Sheepskins, Reawick	B3	40
Silvercraft, Weisdale	B3	40
Sir Walter Scott's Courtroom	B3	14
Skye Watermill	A3	28

Sma' Glen	B2	18
Smokehouse, The	B4	36
Smoo Cave	D1	37
Stenton Fruit Farm	C1	14
Stirling Castle Visitor Centre NTS	B3	18
Storybook Glen	E2	25
Strathisla Distillery	B3	32
Strathspey Railway	E1	23
Struie Viewpoint	D1	31
Stuart Crystal	B2	18
Summer Isles	B4	36
Swannay, Farmhouse Cheese Making (by appt.)	A2	39
Talisker Distillery	B4	28
Tamdhu Distillery	A3	32
Timespan Heritage Centre	A4	38
Tongland Power Station	E3	7
Tormiston Mill	A3	39
Torphichen Preceptory	E1	13
Trumland Pier	B2	39
Tugnet Ice House Exhibition	B2	32
Union Suspension Bridge	D2	15
Uyeasound Knitwear	C1	40
Various Crafts, Eday	B2	39
Various Crafts, Hillswick	B2	40
Various Crafts, Kirkwall	B3	39
Various Crafts, Lerwick	C3	40
Various Crafts, Skallary	E3	27
Various Crafts, South Ronaldsay	B4	39
Vat O' Kirbister	C2	39
Victoria Falls	E2	29
Victoria Park and Fossil Grove	C1	12
Voe Tweed & Knitwear	B3	40
Wade's Bridge	E4	23
Wallace Tower	B3	12
Well of Seven Heads	B2	22
Whiten Head	D1	37
Windyknowe Farm (cheese-making)	A2	8
Wood 'n' Things	E1	7
Woodland Centre	C3	14
Wool Stone	C1	14
Yesnaby Sea Stacks	A3	39

Index to Place Names

Abbreviations used in this Index

Cumbr	Cumbria
D. & G.	Dumfries & Galloway
Grampn	Grampian
Highl	Highland
Lothn	Lothian
Northum	Northumberland
Shetld	Shetland
Strath	Strathclyde
T. & W.	Tyne & Wear
Tays	Tayside
W. Isles	Western Isles

Abbey Town *Cumbr* A3 8
Aberargie *Tays* D2 19
Aberchirder *Grampn* C3 32
Aberdeen *Grampn* E2 25
Aberdour *Fife* D4 19
Aberfeldy *Tays* B1 18
Aberfoyle *Central* A3 18
Aberlady *Lothn* E4 19
Abernethy *Tays* D2 19
Abernyte *Tays* D2 19
Aberuthven *Tays* C2 18
Abington *Strath* E3 13
Aboyne *Grampn* C2 24
Achahoish *Strath* C3 16
Achanalt *Highl* B2 30
Achanamara *Strath* C4 16
Achandunie *Highl* D2 31
Achaphubuil *Highl* A3 22
Acharacle *Highl* E3 21
Achargary *Highl* E2 37
Acharn *Highl* E4 21
Acharn *Tays* B1 18
Acharn *Tays* B3 24
Achavanich *Highl* B3 38
Achentoul *Highl* F3 37
Achfary *Highl* C3 36
Achiemore *Highl* D1 37
Achiemore *Highl* F2 37
Achiltibuie *Highl* B4 36
Achinduich *Highl* C1 30
Achintee *Highl* E3 29
Achlain *Highl* B1 22
Achleck *Strath* A1 16
Achluachrach *Highl* B3 22
Achmore *Highl* E4 29
Achmore *W. Isles* D2 35
Achnaba *Strath* D4 17
Achnacarnin *Highl* B3 36
Achnaclerach *Highl* B2 30
Achnacloich *Highl* D1 21
Achnacraig *Strath* A1 16
Achnadrish *Strath* C4 20
Achnaluachrach *Highl* E4 37
Achnasaul *Highl* B2 22
Achnasheen *Highl* A3 30
Achnashellach Lodge *Highl* E3 29
Achosnich *Highl* C3 20
Achriabhach *Highl* B3 22
Achriesgill *Highl* C2 36
Achtubh *Central* A2 18
Achuvoldrach *Highl* E2 37
Ackergill *Highl* C2 38
Acklington *Northum* F1 9
Adderstone *Northum* E3 15
Advie *Highl* F4 31
Ae *D. & G.* F1 7
Ae Bridgend *D. & G.* F2 7
Affric Lodge *Highl* A4 30
Afton Bridgend *Strath* C4 12
Aimster *Highl* B2 38
Aird *Strath* C3 16
Aird of Sleat *Highl* D2 21
Aird Uig *W. Isles* C2 34
Airdrie *Strath* D1 13
Airth *Central* B4 18
Aith *Shetld* B3 40
Aitnoch *Grampn* E3 31
Akeld *Northum* D3 15
Aldclune *Tays* E4 23
Aldochlay *Strath* F3 17
Alexandria *Strath* F4 17
Alford *Grampn* C1 24
Alladale Lodge *Highl* C1 30
Allanton *Borders* D2 15
Allanton *Strath* D2 13
Allendale Town *Northum* D3 9
Allenheads *Northum* D4 9
Allerwash *Northum* D3 9
Alligin Shuas *Highl* D3 29
Allnabad *Highl* D3 37
Alloa *Central* B3 18
Allonby *Cumbr* A4 8

Alloway *Strath* B4 12
Alltnacaillich *Highl* D2 37
Alness *Highl* D2 31
Alnmouth *Northum* F4 15
Alnwick *Northum* E4 15
Alston *Cumbr* D3 9
Altandhu *Highl* B4 36
Altgaltraig *Strath* F1 11
Alticry *D. & G.* C3 6
Altnacealgach House *Highl* C4 36
Altnafeadh *Highl* B4 22
Altnaharra *Highl* E3 37
Altrua *Highl* B2 22
Alva *Central* B3 18
Alvie *Highl* E1 23
Alyth *Tays* D1 19
Amble *Northum* F4 15
Amisfield *D. & G.* F2 7
Amulree *Tays* B1 18
Anaheilt *Highl* E4 21
Ancroft *Northum* D2 15
Ancrum *Borders* C3 14
Annan *D. & G.* A3 8
Annat *Highl* E3 29
Annat *Strath* D2 17
Annbank *Strath* B3 12
Annbank Station *Strath* B3 12
Annfield Plain *Durham* F3 9
Anstruther Wester *Fife* F3 19
Apperley Dene *Northum* E3 9
Appin House *Strath* D1 17
Applecross *Highl* D3 29
Arbroath *Tays* F1 19
Arbuthnott *Grampn* D3 25
Archiestown *Grampn* B3 32
Ardachvie *Highl* B2 22
Ardbeg *Strath* C2 10
Ardbeg *Strath* E4 17
Ardcharnich *Highl* A1 30
Ardchonnell *Strath* D2 17
Ardchullarie More *Central* A2 18
Ardchyle *Central* A2 18
Ardelve *Highl* E4 29
Arden *Strath* F4 17
Ardentinny *Strath* E4 17
Ardeonaig *Central* A1 18
Ardersier *Highl* D3 31
Ardessie *Highl* E1 29
Ardfern *Strath* C3 16
Ardgay *Highl* C1 30
Ardhasig *W. Isles* C4 34
Ardindrean *Highl* A1 30
Ardivachar *W. Isles* C3 26
Ardjachie *Highl* D1 31
Ardlui *Strath* F2 17
Ardlussa *Strath* B4 16
Ardmair *Highl* F1 29
Ardmay *Strath* E3 17
Ardminish *Strath* D2 11
Ardmolich *Highl* E3 21
Ardnacross *Strath* B1 16
Ardnadam *Strath* E4 17
Ardnastang *Highl* E4 21
Ardnave *Strath* B1 10
Ardpatrick *Strath* D2 11
Ardpeaton *Strath* E4 17
Ardrishaig *Strath* C4 16
Ardroil *W. Isles* C2 34
Ardrossan *Strath* A2 12
Ardscalpsie *Strath* F2 11
Ardshealach *Highl* E3 21
Ardslignish *Highl* D4 21
Ardtalla *Strath* C2 10
Ardtalnaig *Tays* A1 18
Ardtoe *Highl* D3 21
Arduaine *Strath* C3 16
Ardullie Lodge *Highl* C2 30
Ardvasar *Highl* D2 21
Ardvey *W. Isles* C4 34
Ardvourlie Castle *W. Isles* C3 34
Ardwell *D. & G.* B3 6
Ardwell *Strath* B1 6
Aribruach *W. Isles* D3 35
Arichastlich *Strath* E1 17
Aridhglas *Strath* A2 16
Arinagour *Strath* B4 20
Arisaig *Highl* D2 21
Armadale *Lothn* E1 13
Armadale Castle *Highl* D2 21
Arnabost *Strath* B4 20
Arnisdale *Highl* E1 21
Arnol *W. Isles* D1 35
Arnprior *Central* A3 18
Aros Mains *Strath* B1 16
Arrochar *Strath* E3 17
Artafallie *Highl* C3 30
Ascog *Strath* F2 11
Ashgill Head *Durham* D4 9
Ashington *Northum* F2 9

Ashkirk *Borders* B3 14
Ashybank *Borders* B4 14
Aspatria *Cumbr* A4 8
Athelstaneford *Lothn* B1 14
Auchallater *Grampn* A2 24
Aucharnie *Grampn* D3 33
Aucharrigill *Highl* D4 37
Auchbraad *Strath* C4 16
Auchenblae *Grampn* D3 25
Auchenbrack *D. & G.* E1 7
Auchenbreck *Strath* D4 17
Auchencairn *D. & G.* E3 7
Auchencrow *Borders* D2 15
Auchendinny *Lothn* A2 14
Auchenheath *Strath* D2 13
Auchenlarie *D. & G.* D3 7
Auchenmalg Bridge *D. & G.* B3 6
Auchentiber *Strath* B2 12
Auchgourish *Highl* E1 23
Auchindrain *Strath* D3 17
Auchinhove *Grampn* C3 32
Auchinleck *Strath* C3 12
Auchintore *Highl* A3 22
Auchiries *Grampn* F4 33
Auchleven *Grampn* C4 32
Auchmuirbridge *Tays* D3 19
Auchnacraig *Strath* C2 16
Auchnagatt *Grampn* E3 33
Aucholzie *Grampn* B2 24
Auchterarder *Tays* C2 18
Auchterderran *Fife* D3 19
Auchterhouse *Tays* D1 19
Auchtermuchty *Fife* D3 19
Auchtertool *Fife* D3 19
Auckingill *Highl* C2 38
Auldearn *Highl* E3 31
Auldgirth *D. & G.* F2 7
Auldhame *Lothn* F4 19
Aulich *Tays* D4 23
Ault-a-chruinn *Highl* F1 21
Aultbea *Highl* E1 29
Aultbeg *Grampn* B4 32
Aultdearg *Highl* B2 30
Aultgrishan *Highl* D1 29
Aultguish Inn *Highl* B2 30
Aultmore *Grampn* B3 32
Aultnamain Inn *Highl* D2 31
Avielochan *Highl* E1 23
Aviemore *Highl* E1 23
Avoch *Highl* D3 31
Avonbridge *Central* E1 13
Awhirk *D. & G.* B3 6
Aydon *Northum* E3 9
Ayr *Strath* B3 12
Ayton *Borders* D2 15
Back *W. Isles* E2 35
Backaland *Orkney* B2 39
Backhill *Grampn* E3 33
Backworth *T. & W.* F2 9
Badachro *Highl* D2 29
Badanloch Lodge *Highl* F3 37
Badcall *Highl* C2 36
Badcaul *Highl* E1 29
Badenscoth *Grampn* D3 33
Badenyon *Grampn* B1 24
Badintagairt *Highl* D4 37
Badlipster *Highl* B2 38
Badrallach *Highl* F1 29
Baile Boidheach *Strath* D1 11
Baile Mor *Strath* A2 16
Bailivanish *W. Isles* C3 26
Bainshole *Grampn* C4 32
Balallan *W. Isles* D3 35
Balbeggie *Tays* D2 19
Balblair *Highl* C1 30
Balblair *Highl* D2 31
Balchladich *Highl* B3 36
Baldinnie *Fife* E3 19
Baldovie *Fife* E1 19
Balephuil *Strath* A1 20
Balerno *Lothn* F1 13
Balfour *Orkney* B3 39
Balfron *Central* A4 18
Balgedie *Tays* D3 19
Balgowan *Highl* D2 23
Balgown *Highl* B2 28
Balgrochan *Strath* A4 18
Balgy *Highl* E3 29
Balintore *Highl* E2 31
Ballachulish *Highl* A4 22
Ballaglasa *W. Isles* C2 26
Ballantrae *Strath* B2 6
Ballantrushal *W. Isles* D1 35
Ballater *Grampn* B2 24
Ballcorach *Grampn* A4 32
Ballencrieff *Lothn* E1 19
Balliemore *Strath* C2 16
Ballinluig *Tays* F4 23
Ballintuim *Tays* A4 24

Balloch *Strath*	F4	17
Ballochan *Grampn*	C2	24
Ballochmorrie *Strath*	B2	6
Ballochroy *Strath*	D2	11
Ballogie *Grampn*	C2	24
Ballygown *Strath*	A1	16
Ballygrant *Strath*	C1	10
Ballyhaugh *Strath*	B4	20
Ballymichael *Strath*	E3	11
Balmacara *Highl*	D4	29
Balmaclellan *D. & G.*	D2	7
Balmacneil *Tays*	F4	23
Balmaha *Central*	F3	17
Balmedie *Grampn*	E1	25
Balminnoch *D. & G.*	C3	6
Balmore *Highl*	B4	30
Balmore *Strath*	C1	12
Balmore *W. Isles*	B3	26
Balmule *Fife*	D4	19
Balmullo *Fife*	E2	19
Balnabodach *W. Isles*	E3	27
Balnaboth *Tays*	B3	24
Balnabruich *Highl*	B3	38
Balnacoil Lodge *Highl*	F4	37
Balnacra *Highl*	E3	29
Balnacraig *Highl*	C2	30
Balnafoich *Highl*	D4	31
Balnagall *Highl*	D2	31
Balnaguard *Tays*	E4	23
Balnaha *Highl*	E2	31
Balnahard *Strath*	A1	16
Balnakeil *Highl*	D1	37
Balnapaling *Highl*	D2	31
Balquhidder *Central*	A2	18
Baltasound *Shetld*	C1	40
Balvicar *Strath*	C2	16
Bamburgh *Northum*	E3	15
Banchory *Grampn*	D2	25
Banff *Grampn*	D2	33
Bankend *D. & G.*	F2	7
Bankfoot *Tays*	C1	18
Bankglen *Strath*	C4	12
Banks *Orkney*	B2	39
Bankshill *D. & G.*	A2	8
Bannockburn *Central*	B4	18
Barassie *Strath*	B3	12
Barbaraville *Highl*	D2	31
Barcaldine *Strath*	D1	17
Bardon Mill *Northum*	D3	9
Bargrennan *D. & G.*	C2	6
Barharrow *D. & G.*	D3	7
Barlae *D. & G.*	C3	6
Barmurrie *D. & G.*	E2	7
Barnacarry *Strath*	D3	17
Barnbarroch *D. & G.*	E3	7
Barr *Strath*	C1	6
Barrahormid *Strath*	C4	16
Barravullin *Strath*	C3	16
Barrhead *Strath*	C2	12
Barrhill *Strath*	B2	6
Barrmill *Strath*	B2	12
Barrowburn *Northum*	D4	15
Barry *Tays*	E1	19
Barvas *W. Isles*	D1	35
Bassenfell *Cumbr*	A4	8
Bathgate *Lothn*	E1	13
Bayhead *W. Isles*	B3	26
Bayles *Cumbr*	D4	9
Beadnell *Northum*	F3	15
Beal *Northum*	E2	15
Bearsbridge *Northum*	D3	9
Bearsden *Strath*	C1	12
Beattock *D. & G.*	A1	7
Beauly *Highl*	C3	30
Bebside *Northum*	F2	9
Beckfoot *Cumbr*	A3	8
Bedlington *Northum*	F2	9
Beeswing *D. & G.*	F2	7
Beith *Strath*	B2	12
Belford *Northum*	E3	15
Belhinnie *Grampn*	C4	32
Bellabeg *Grampn*	B1	24
Bellanoch *Strath*	C3	16
Belle Vue *Cumbr*	A4	8
Bellehiglash *Grampn*	A4	32
Bellingham *Northum*	D2	9
Belloch *Strath*	D3	11
Bellochantuy *Strath*	D3	11
Bellshill *Northum*	E3	15
Bellshill *Strath*	D2	13
Bellspool *Borders*	F3	13
Bellsquarry *Lothn*	E1	13
Bellymack *D. & G.*	E3	7
Belnacraig *Grampn*	B1	24
Belsay *Northum*	F2	9
Belses *Borders*	B3	14
Belston *Strath*	B3	12
Ben Armine Lodge *Highl*	E4	37
Benalder Lodge *Highl*	D3	23
Benderloch *Strath*	D1	17
Bendronaig Lodge *Highl*	E4	29
Benfield *D. & G.*	C3	6
Bennan *Strath*	F3	11
Bennecarrigan *Strath*	E3	11
Bentpath *D. & G.*	B1	8
Beoraidbeg *Highl*	E2	21
Bernera *Highl*	E1	21
Bernisdale *Highl*	B3	28
Berriedale *Highl*	B3	38
Berryhillock *Grampn*	C2	32
Berryscaur *D. & G.*	A1	8
Berwick-upon-Tweed *Northum*	D2	15
Bettyhill *Highl*	E2	37
Bewaldeth *Cumbr*	A4	8
Bieldside *Grampn*	E2	25
Big Balcraig *D. & G.*	C4	6
Big Corlae *D. & G.*	D1	7
Biggar *Strath*	E3	13
Bilbster *Highl*	B2	38
Binniehill *Central*	D1	13
Birdston *Strath*	C1	12
Birgham *Borders*	C3	14
Birkenhills *Grampn*	D3	33
Birkhill *D. & G.*	F4	13
Birkhill *Tays*	D1	19
Birling *Northum*	F4	15
Birnam *Tays*	C1	18
Birsemore *Grampn*	C2	24
Birtley *T. & W.*	F3	9
Bishop Auckland *Durham*	F4	9
Bishopbriggs *Strath*	C1	12
Bishopton *D. & G.*	C4	6
Bishopton *Strath*	B1	12
Bitterlees *Cumbr*	A3	8
Bixter *Shetld*	B3	40
Black Heddon *Northum*	E2	9
Blackacre *D. & G.*	F1	7
Blackadder *Borders*	D2	15
Blackburn *Grampn*	D1	25
Blackburn *Lothn*	E1	13
Blackburn *Strath*	D3	13
Blackford *Cumbr*	B3	8
Blackford *Tays*	B3	18
Blackhaugh *Borders*	B3	14
Blackhill *Grampn*	F3	33
Blackhill *Highl*	B3	28
Blackhillock *Grampn*	B3	32
Blacklaw *D. & G.*	E4	13
Blackness *Lothn*	C4	18
Blackridge *Lothn*	D1	13
Blackrock *Strath*	B1	10
Blackwaterfoot *Strath*	E3	11
Blackwood *D. & G.*	F2	7
Bladnoch *D. & G.*	C3	6
Blagill *Cumbr*	D3	9
Blaich *Highl*	A3	22
Blair Atholl *Tays*	E3	23
Blairgowrie *Tays*	D1	19
Blairingone *Tays*	C3	18
Blairmore *Highl*	C2	36
Blairnamarrow *Grampn*	A1	24
Blairquhosh *Central*	A4	18
Blairydryne *Grampn*	D2	25
Blakelaw *Borders*	C3	14
Blanchland *Durham*	E3	9
Blanefield *Central*	A4	18
Blarghour *Strath*	D2	17
Blarmachfoldach *Highl*	A3	22
Blarnaleyoch *Highl*	A1	30
Blaydon *T. & W.*	F3	9
Blyth Bridge *Borders*	F2	13
Bo'ness *Central*	C4	18
Boardhouse *Orkney*	A2	39
Boarhills *Fife*	F2	19
Boat of Garten *Highl*	E1	23
Boddam *Grampn*	F3	33
Bogallan *Highl*	D3	31
Bogbrae *Grampn*	E3	33
Bogend *Borders*	C2	14
Bogend *Strath*	B3	12
Boghall *Lothn*	E1	13
Boghall *Lothn*	F1	13
Boghall *Strath*	B4	12
Bogmuir *Grampn*	B2	32
Bogniebrae *Grampn*	C3	32
Bogroy *Highl*	E4	31
Bogside *Strath*	D2	13
Bogue *D. & G.*	D2	7
Bohuntine *Highl*	B3	22
Boleside *Borders*	B3	14
Bolton *Lothn*	B1	14
Bolton Low Houses *Cumbr*	A4	8
Boltongate *Cumbr*	A4	8
Bonar Bridge *Highl*	C1	30
Bonawe *Strath*	D1	17
Bonchester Bridge *Borders*	B4	14
Bonhill *Strath*	F4	17
Bonjedward *Borders*	C3	14
Bonnybank *Fife*	E3	13
Bonnybridge *Central*	B4	18
Bonnyrigg *Lothn*	A1	14
Boquhan *Central*	A4	18
Boreland *D. & G.*	A1	8
Borgie *Highl*	E2	37
Borgue *D. & G.*	D3	7
Borgue *Highl*	B3	38
Borve *Highl*	C3	28
Borve *W. Isles*	B2	26
Borve *W. Isles*	E3	27
Bothel *Cumbr*	A4	8
Bothwell *Strath*	D2	13
Boultenstone *Grampn*	B1	24
Bousd *Strath*	C4	20
Bow *Borders*	B2	14
Bow *Orkney*	B3	39
Bow of Fife *Fife*	D2	19
Bowburn *Durham*	F4	9
Bowden *Borders*	B3	14
Bowmore *Strath*	B2	10
Bowside Lodge *Highl*	F2	37
Bowtrees *Central*	B4	18
Brabster *Highl*	C1	38
Bracadale *Highl*	B4	28
Brackley *Highl*	D3	31
Braco *Tays*	B3	18
Bracorina *Highl*	E2	21
Brae *Shetld*	B2	40
Brae Roy Lodge *Highl*	C2	22
Braeantra *Highl*	C2	30
Braefield *Highl*	B4	30
Braegrum *Tays*	C2	18
Braehead *Strath*	E2	13
Braehungie *Highl*	B3	38
Braemar *Grampn*	A2	24
Braemore *Highl*	A2	30
Braemore *Highl*	A3	38
Braes of Ullapool *Highl*	A1	30
Braeside *Strath*	A1	12
Braeswick *Orkney*	B2	39
Bragar *W. Isles*	D1	35
Brampton *Cumbr*	C3	8
Branault *Highl*	D3	21
Brancepeth *Durham*	F4	9
Branderburgh *Grampn*	B2	32
Brandon *Durham*	F4	9
Branxholme *Borders*	B4	14
Brawlbin *Highl*	A2	38
Breasclete *W. Isles*	C2	34
Brechin *Tays*	C4	24
Breich *Lothn*	E2	13
Bremirehoull *Shetld*	B4	40
Brenish *W. Isles*	B2	34
Brewlands Bridge *Tays*	A4	24
Bridge of Alford *Grampn*	C1	24
Bridge of Allan *Central*	B3	18
Bridge of Avon *Grampn*	A4	32
Bridge of Awe *Strath*	D2	17
Bridge of Brown *Highl*	A1	24
Bridge of Cally *Tays*	A4	24
Bridge of Canny *Grampn*	D2	25
Bridge of Dee *D. & G.*	E3	7
Bridge of Don *Grampn*	E1	25
Bridge of Dye *Grampn*	D3	25
Bridge of Earn *Tays*	C2	18
Bridge of Ericht *Tays*	C4	22
Bridge of Feugh *Grampn*	D2	25
Bridge of Forss *Highl*	A1	38
Bridge of Gairn *Grampn*	B2	24
Bridge of Gaur *Tays*	C4	22
Bridge of Orchy *Strath*	E1	17
Bridge of Weir *Strath*	B1	12
Bridgefoot *Cumbr*	F4	7
Bridgend *Grampn*	B4	32
Bridgend *Grampn*	E4	33
Bridgend *Strath*	C2	10
Bridgend *Strath*	C3	16
Bridgend *Tays*	C2	18
Bridgend *Tays*	C3	24
Bridgend of Mountblairy *Grampn*	D3	33
Brig o'Turk *Central*	A3	18
Brigham *Cumbr*	A4	8
Brightons *Central*	E1	13
Brinyan *Orkney*	B2	39
Broadford *Highl*	D4	29
Broadmeadows *Borders*	B3	14
Broats *D. & G.*	A2	8
Brochel *Highl*	C3	28
Brodick *Strath*	F3	11
Brogaig *Highl*	C2	28
Broom *Durham*	F4	9
Broomhaugh *Northum*	E3	9
Broomhill *Northum*	F1	9
Brora *Highl*	F4	37
Brough *Highl*	B1	38
Brough *Shetld*	B2	40

Brough *Shetld* C2 40
Broughton *Borders* E3 13
Broughty Ferry *Tays* E2 19
Brownhill *Grampn* E3 33
Brownyside *Northum* E3 15
Broxburn *Lothn* C1 14
Broxburn *Lothn* E1 13
Bruichladdich *Strath* B2 10
Bruist *W. Isles* A2 26
Buchanty *Tays* B2 18
Buchlyvie *Central* A3 18
Buckabank *Cumbr* B3 8
Buckhaven *Fife* E3 19
Buckholm *Borders* B3 14
Buckie *Grampn* B2 32
Bucksburn *Grampn* E1 25
Buckton *Northum* E3 15
Budle *Northum* E3 15
Buldoo *Highl* A1 38
Bullwood *Strath* A1 12
Bunacaimb *Highl* D2 21
Bunarkaig *Highl* B2 22
Bunaveneadar *W. Isles* C3 34
Bunessan *Strath* A2 16
Burg *Strath* A1 16
Burghead *Grampn* F2 31
Burnfoot *D. & G.* F1 7
Burnhaven *Grampn* F3 33
Burnhead *D. & G.* E1 7
Burnhouse *Strath* B2 12
Burnmouth *Borders* D2 15
Burnopfield *Durham* F3 9
Burnside *Fife* D3 19
Burnside *Strath* C4 12
Burnside *Tays* C4 24
Burntisland *Fife* D4 19
Burradon *T. & W.* F2 9
Burravoe *Shetld* C2 40
Burrelton *Tays* D1 19
Burwick *Orkney* B4 39
Busby *Strath* C2 12
Bush Lawsie *Grampn* B2 24
Butterknowle *Durham* F4 9
Butterstone *Tays* C1 18
Byrness *Northum* D1 9
Cabrach *Grampn* B4 32
Cabuie Lodge *Highl* A2 30
Caddonfoot *Borders* B3 14
Cairnbaan *Strath* C3 16
Cairncross *Borders* D1 15
Cairncross *Tays* C3 24
Cairncurran *Strath* B1 12
Cairndow *Strath* E3 17
Cairneyhill *Fife* C4 18
Cairnhill *Grampn* D4 33
Cairnie *Grampn* D2 25
Cairnoch *Central* A4 18
Cairnorrie *Grampn* E3 33
Cairnryan *D. & G.* B2 6
Cairntable *Strath* B4 12
Cairnwhin *Strath* B1 6
Caitha *Borders* B3 14
Calcots *Grampn* B2 32
Caldbeck *Cumbr* B4 8
Caldercruix *Strath* D1 13
Caldermill *Strath* C3 12
Calgary *Strath* C4 20
Calgow *D. & G.* C3 6
California *Central* D1 13
Callaly *Northum* E4 15
Callander *Central* A3 18
Callert *Highl* A4 22
Calvine *Tays* E3 23
Calvo *Cumbr* A3 8
Calzeat *Borders* E3 13
Camasinas *Highl* D4 21
Camasine *Highl* E4 21
Camasnacroise *Highl* E4 21
Camb *Shetld* C1 40
Cambo *Northum* E2 9
Cambus o'May *Grampn* B2 24
Cambuslang *Strath* C2 12
Cambusmore Lodge *Highl* D1 31
Camelon *Central* B4 18
Camghouran *Tays* D4 23
Cammachmore *Grampn* E2 25
Campbeltown *Strath* D3 11
Camperdown *T. & W.* F2 9
Camptown *Borders* C4 14
Camusdarrach *Highl* D2 21
Camusnagaul *Highl* F1 29
Camusterrach *Highl* D3 29
Camusvrachan *Tays* D4 23
Cannich *Highl* B4 30
Canonbie *D. & G.* B2 8
Caol *Highl* A3 22
Caoles *Strath* A1 20
Cappercleuch *Borders* F3 13

Capplegill *D. & G.* F4 13
Caputh *Tays* C1 18
Carbost *Highl* B4 28
Carbost *Highl* C3 28
Cardenden *Fife* D3 19
Cardow *Grampn* A3 32
Cardrona *Borders* A3 14
Cardross *Strath* B1 12
Carfin *Strath* D2 13
Cargenbridge *D. & G.* F2 7
Cargill *Tays* D1 19
Carham *Northum* D3 15
Carie *Tays* D4 23
Carlisle *Cumbr* B3 8
Carlops *Borders* F2 13
Carloway *W. Isles* C2 34
Carluke *Strath* D2 13
Carmacoup *Strath* D3 13
Carmunnock *Strath* C2 12
Carmyllie *Tays* E1 19
Carnach *Highl* E4 29
Carnachy *Highl* E2 37
Carnan *W. Isles* C2 26
Carnbo *Tays* C3 18
Carnoch *Highl* B3 30
Carnock *Fife* C4 18
Carnoustie *Tays* F1 19
Carnwath *Strath* E2 13
Carradale *Strath* E3 11
Carrbridge *Highl* E4 31
Carrick *Fife* E2 19
Carrick *Orkney* B2 39
Carrick *Strath* E3 17
Carron Bridge *Central* E1 7
Carronbridge *D. & G.* E1 7
Carrutherstown *D. & G.* A2 8
Carsaig *Strath* B2 16
Carsegown *D. & G.* C3 6
Carskiey *Strath* D4 11
Carsluith *D. & G.* D3 7
Carsphairn *D. & G.* D1 7
Carstairs *Strath* E2 13
Carter Bar *Borders* C4 14
Cartington *Northum* E4 15
Cashlie *Tays* F1 17
Castle Carrock *Cumbr* C3 8
Castle Douglas *D. & G.* E3 7
Castle O'er *D. & G.* A1 8
Castle Stuart *Highl* D3 31
Castlebay *W. Isles* E3 27
Castlefairn *D. & G.* E2 7
Castlehill *D. & G.* F2 7
Castleside *Durham* E3 9
Castleton *Borders* C1 8
Castleton *Strath* C4 16
Castleton *Tays* D1 19
Castletown *Highl* B1 38
Catacol *Strath* E2 11
Catcleugh *Northum* D1 9
Caterway Heads *Northum* E3 9
Catlowdy *Cumbr* B2 8
Catrine *Strath* C3 12
Catton *Northum* D3 9
Cauldhame *Central* A3 18
Cauldside *D. & G.* B2 8
Cauldwells *Grampn* D3 33
Caulkerbush *D. & G.* F3 7
Causeway End *D. & G.* C3 6
Causewayend *Strath* E3 13
Causewayhead *Central* B3 18
Causewayhead *Cumbr* A3 8
Cawdor *Highl* E3 31
Ceres *Fife* E3 19
Cessford *Borders* C3 14
Challoch *D. & G.* C2 6
Champany *Central* C4 18
Chapel *D. & G.* E3 7
Chapel Hill *Grampn* F4 33
Chapel Rossan *D. & G.* B4 6
Chapelhall *Strath* D1 13
Chapelhill *Highl* D2 31
Chapelhill *Tays* C2 18
Chapelhill *Tays* D2 19
Chapelknowe *D. & G.* B2 8
Chapelton *Strath* C2 12
Chapelton *Tays* F1 19
Chapelton *Tays* C4 24
Charleston *Tays* E1 19
Charlestown *Grampn* E2 25
Charlestown *Highl* D2 29
Charlestown of Aberlour B3 32
  Grampn
Charlton Mires *Northum* E3 15
Chatto *Borders* C4 14
Chatton *Northum* E3 15
Chealamy *Highl* E2 37
Cheeklaw *Borders* C2 14
Chester Moor *Durham* F3 9
Chester-le-Street *Durham* F3 9

Chesters *Borders* C4 14
Chirmorie *Strath* B2 6
Chirnside *Borders* D2 15
Chirnsidebridge *Borders* D2 15
Choicelee *Borders* C2 14
Christon Bank *Northum* E3 15
Clachaig *Strath* E4 17
Clachan *Strath* C1 16
Clachan *Strath* C2 16
Clachan *Strath* E2 11
Clachan *Strath* E2 17
Clachan *Tays* E3 23
Clachan *W. Isles* B2 26
Clachan Mor *Strath* A1 20
Clachan of Glendaruel D4 17
  Strath
Clachan-Seil *Strath* C2 16
Clachbreck *Strath* E1 11
Clachnabrain *Tays* B3 24
Clachtoll *Highl* B3 36
Clackmannan *Central* B3 18
Cladich *Strath* E2 17
Claggan *Highl* C1 16
Claonaig *Strath* E2 11
Clarencefield *D. & G.* A2 8
Clarilaw *Borders* B4 14
Clarkston *Strath* C2 12
Clashmore *Highl* D1 31
Clashnessie *Highl* B3 36
Clatt *Grampn* C4 32
Clatterin Brig *Grampn* D3 25
Clatteringshaws *D. & G.* D2 7
Cleadale *Highl* D2 21
Cleat *Orkney* B4 39
Clephanton *Highl* D3 31
Clerklands *Borders* B3 14
Cleuchbrae *D. & G.* F2 7
Clifton *Central* F2 17
Clifton *Cumbr* C4 8
Clifton *Northum* F2 9
Climpy *Strath* E2 13
Clola *Grampn* E3 33
Closeburn *D. & G.* F1 7
Clova *Tays* B3 24
Clovenfords *Borders* B3 14
Clovulin *Highl* F4 21
Cluanie Inn *Highl* A1 22
Clydebank *Strath* C1 12
Clynder *Strath* E4 17
Clyth *Highl* B3 38
Coalfell *Cumbr* C3 8
Coalhall *Strath* B4 12
Coaltown of Wemyss *Fife* D3 19
Coast *Highl* E1 29
Coatbridge *Strath* D1 13
Coburty *Grampn* E2 33
Cock Bridge *Grampn* B1 24
Cockburnspath *Borders* C1 14
Cockenzie *Lothn* B1 14
Cockermouth *Cumbr* A4 8
Coignafearn Lodge *Highl* D1 23
Coilantogle *Central* A3 18
Coille Mhorgil *Highl* A2 22
Coillore *Highl* B4 28
Colaboll *Highl* E4 37
Colbost *Highl* A3 28
Coldbackie *Highl* E2 37
Coldingham *Borders* D1 15
Coldstream *Borders* D3 15
Coldwells *Grampn* F4 33
Colgrain *Strath* F4 17
Colinsburgh *Fife* E3 19
Colinton *Lothn* F1 13
Colintraive *Strath* F1 11
Coll *W. Isles* E2 35
Collafirth *Shetld* B2 40
Collieston *Grampn* E4 33
Collin *D. & G.* F2 7
Colliston *Tays* F1 19
Colmonel *Strath* B2 6
Colnabaichin *Grampn* B1 24
Colpy *Grampn* D4 33
Colquhar *Borders* A2 14
Colvend *D. & G.* E3 7
Comrie *Fife* C4 18
Comrie *Tays* B2 18
Conchra *Strath* D4 17
Condorrat *Strath* D1 13
Congash *Highl* F4 31
Connel *Strath* D1 17
Connel Park *Strath* C4 12
Conon Bridge *Highl* C3 30
Consett *Durham* F3 9
Contin *Highl* C3 30
Copister *Shetld* C2 40
Copley *Durham* E4 9
Corbridge *Northum* E3 9
Cornhill *Grampn* C3 32
Cornhill-on-Tweed *Northum* D3 15

Place	Ref	Page
Corpach *Highl*	A3	22
Corran *Highl*	A4	22
Corran *Highl*	E1	21
Corranbuie *Strath*	E1	11
Corribeg *Highl*	A3	22
Corrie *Strath*	F2	11
Corriegour *Highl*	B2	22
Corriemoillie *Highl*	B2	30
Corrievorrie *Highl*	D4	31
Corry *Highl*	D4	29
Corrymuckloch *Tays*	B1	18
Corsock *D. & G.*	E2	7
Cortachy *Tays*	B4	24
Cot-town *Grampn*	D3	33
Cothall *Grampn*	E1	25
Coulags *Highl*	E3	29
Coulport *Strath*	E4	17
Coulter *Strath*	E3	13
Coundon *Durham*	F4	9
Coupar Angus *Tays*	D1	19
Cove *Highl*	D1	29
Cove *Strath*	E4	17
Covesea *Grampn*	A2	32
Cowdenbeath *Fife*	D3	19
Cowdenburn *Borders*	F2	13
Cowie *Central*	B4	18
Cowshill *Durham*	D4	9
Cowstrandburn *Fife*	C3	18
Coylton *Strath*	B4	12
Coylumbridge *Highl*	E1	23
Crackaig *Highl*	A4	38
Craggan *Grampn*	A4	32
Craichie *Tays*	E1	19
Craig *Highl*	E3	29
Craig *Strath*	C1	6
Craig Castle *Grampn*	C4	32
Craigbeg *Highl*	C3	22
Craigdarroch *Strath*	C4	12
Craigdews *D. & G.*	D2	7
Craigellachie *Grampn*	B3	32
Craigencross *D. & G.*	A3	6
Craigend *Tays*	C2	18
Craigendoran *Strath*	F4	17
Craigenrae *Strath*	C1	6
Craighat *Central*	F4	17
Craighouse *Strath*	C1	10
Craiglemine *D. & G.*	C4	6
Craiglug *Grampn*	D2	25
Craigmaud *Grampn*	E3	33
Craigmore *Strath*	F1	11
Craignure *Strath*	C1	16
Craigrothie *Fife*	E3	19
Craigruie *Central*	F2	17
Craigs, The *Highl*	C1	30
Craigton *Grampn*	D2	25
Craigton *Tays*	E1	19
Craigton *Tays*	B4	24
Craigtown *Highl*	F2	37
Crail *Fife*	F3	19
Crailing *Borders*	C3	14
Cramalt *Borders*	F3	13
Cramlington *Northum*	F2	9
Cramond Bridge *Lothn*	F1	13
Cranshaws *Borders*	C2	14
Crarae *Strath*	D3	17
Crask Inn *Highl*	D3	37
Crask of Aigas *Highl*	C3	30
Craskins *Grampn*	C2	24
Craster *Northum*	F4	15
Crathie *Grampn*	B2	24
Crawcrook *T. & W.*	F3	9
Crawfordjohn *Strath*	D3	13
Crawick *D. & G.*	D4	13
Crawley Side *Durham*	E4	9
Cray *Tays*	A4	24
Creagan *Strath*	D1	17
Creagorry *W. Isles*	C2	26
Creeside *Strath*	C2	6
Creetown *D. & G.*	D3	7
Creggans *Strath*	D3	17
Crelevan *Highl*	B4	30
Cretshengan *Strath*	D1	11
Crianlarich *Central*	F2	17
Crichton *Lothn*	B2	14
Crieff *Tays*	B2	18
Crimond *Grampn*	E3	33
Crinan *Strath*	C3	16
Crocketford or Ninemile Bar *D. & G.*	E2	7
Croftamie *Central*	F4	17
Crofts *Grampn*	B3	32
Croggan *Strath*	C2	16
Croglin *Cumbr*	C3	8
Croir *W. Isles*	C2	34
Cromarty *Highl*	D2	31
Cromasag *Highl*	E3	29
Cromdale *Highl*	F4	31
Cromore *W. Isles*	D3	35
Cronberry *Strath*	C3	12
Crook *Durham*	F4	9
Crook of Alves *Grampn*	F2	31
Crook of Devon *Tays*	C3	18
Crookham *Northum*	D3	15
Crookhaugh *Borders*	E3	13
Crosby *Cumbr*	A4	8
Crosby Villa *Cumbr*	A4	8
Cross *W. Isles*	E1	35
Crossaig *Strath*	E2	11
Crossbost *W. Isles*	D3	35
Crossford *Fife*	C4	18
Crossford *Strath*	D2	13
Crossgates *Fife*	D4	19
Crosshands *Strath*	B3	12
Crosshill *Strath*	B4	12
Crosshouse *Strath*	B3	12
Crossings *Cumbr*	C2	8
Crosslee *Borders*	A4	14
Crossmichael *D. & G.*	E3	7
Crossroads *Strath*	B3	12
Crows *D. & G.*	C3	6
Croxdale *Durham*	F4	9
Croy *Highl*	D3	31
Croy *Strath*	D1	13
Crubenmore Lodge *Highl*	D2	23
Cruden Bay *Grampn*	F4	33
Crulivig *W. Isles*	C2	34
Culbokie *Highl*	C3	30
Culcabock *Highl*	D3	31
Culdrain *Grampn*	C4	32
Culduie *Highl*	D3	29
Culgaith *Cumbr*	C4	8
Culkein *Highl*	B3	36
Cullen *Grampn*	C2	32
Cullerlie *Grampn*	D2	25
Cullicudden *Highl*	D2	31
Cullipool *Strath*	C2	16
Cullivoe *Shetld*	C1	40
Culloch *Tays*	B2	18
Culmaily *Highl*	D1	31
Culmalzie *D. & G.*	C3	6
Culnacraig *Highl*	B4	36
Culnaknock *Highl*	C2	28
Culross *Fife*	C4	18
Culroy *Strath*	B4	12
Culswick *Shetld*	B3	40
Cults *D. & G.*	D4	6
Cults *Grampn*	E2	25
Cumbernauld *Strath*	D1	13
Cuminestown *Grampn*	D3	33
Cummertrees *D. & G.*	A3	8
Cummingstown *Grampn*	F2	31
Cumnock *Strath*	C4	12
Cumwhinton *Cumbr*	B3	8
Cupar *Fife*	E2	19
Currie *Lothn*	F1	13
Daddry Shield *Durham*	E4	9
Dailly *Strath*	C1	6
Dairsie or Osnaburgh *Fife*	E2	19
Dalavich *Strath*	D2	17
Dalbeattie *D. & G.*	E3	7
Dalbreck *Highl*	E4	37
Dalchalloch *Tays*	D4	23
Dalchalm *Highl*	F4	37
Dalchork *Highl*	E4	37
Dalchruin *Tays*	A2	18
Dalgarven *Strath*	B2	12
Dalginross *Tays*	B2	18
Dalguise *Tays*	C1	18
Dalhalvaig *Highl*	F2	37
Daliburgh *W. Isles*	D3	27
Dalinlongart *Strath*	E4	17
Dalkeith *Lothn*	A1	14
Dallas *Grampn*	F3	31
Dalleagles *Strath*	C4	12
Dalmally *Strath*	E2	17
Dalmellington *Strath*	B4	12
Dalmichy *Highl*	E4	37
Dalmore *Highl*	D2	31
Dalnabreck *Highl*	E3	21
Dalnacardoch Lodge *Tays*	D3	23
Dalnaclach *Highl*	D2	31
Dalnaspidal Lodge *Tays*	D3	23
Dalnavie *Highl*	D2	31
Dalnawillan Lodge *Highl*	A3	38
Dalness *Strath*	B4	22
Dalreavoch *Highl*	E4	37
Dalry *Strath*	B2	12
Dalrymple *Strath*	B4	12
Dalserf *Strath*	D2	13
Dalston *Cumbr*	B3	8
Dalton *D. & G.*	A2	8
Daltot *Strath*	C4	16
Dalvadie *D. & G.*	B3	6
Dalveich *Central*	A2	18
Dalvina Lodge *Highl*	E2	37
Dalwhinnie *Highl*	D3	23
Damnaglaur *D. & G.*	B4	6
Damside *Borders*	F2	13
Dandaleith *Grampn*	B3	32
Danskine *Lothn*	B1	14
Darra *Grampn*	D3	33
Darvel *Strath*	C3	12
Davington *D. & G.*	A1	8
Daviot *Highl*	D4	31
Davoch of Grange *Grampn*	C3	32
Deadwaters *Strath*	D2	13
Deanich Lodge *Highl*	B1	30
Dechmont *Lothn*	E1	13
Deecastle *Grampn*	C2	24
Delchirach *Grampn*	A4	32
Dell *Grampn*	A4	32
Dell *W. Isles*	E1	35
Delliefure *Highl*	F4	31
Den, The *Strath*	B2	12
Denhead *Grampn*	E3	33
Denholm *Borders*	B4	14
Denny *Central*	B4	18
Dennyloanhead *Central*	B4	18
Denwick *Northum*	E4	15
Derryguaig *Strath*	B1	16
Dervaig *Strath*	C4	20
Digg *Highl*	C2	28
Dilston *Northum*	E3	9
Dingwall *Highl*	C3	30
Dinnet *Grampn*	C2	24
Dinvin *D. & G.*	A3	6
Dinwoodiegreen *D. & G.*	A2	8
Dippen *Strath*	E3	11
Dipple *Strath*	B1	6
Dippon *Strath*	F3	11
Dirdhu *Highl*	F1	23
Dirlet *Lothn*	E4	19
Dirt Pot *Northum*	D3	9
Dochfour House *Highl*	C4	30
Dochgarroch *Highl*	C3	30
Doddington *Northum*	D3	15
Dollar *Central*	C3	18
Dolphinton *Strath*	E2	13
Doonfoot *Strath*	B4	12
Dores *Highl*	C4	30
Dornie *Highl*	E4	29
Dornoch *Highl*	D1	31
Dornock *D. & G.*	A3	8
Dougarie *Strath*	E3	11
Douglas *Strath*	D3	13
Douglastown *Tays*	E1	19
Dounby *Orkney*	A2	39
Doune *Central*	B3	18
Dounepark *Strath*	B1	6
Dounie *Highl*	C1	30
Dovenby *Cumbr*	A4	8
Dowally *Tays*	C1	18
Downfield *Tays*	E2	19
Downhill *Tays*	C2	18
Drakemyre *Strath*	B2	12
Dreghorn *Strath*	B3	12
Drem *Lothn*	E4	19
Drimnin *Highl*	D4	21
Drimsallie *Highl*	F3	21
Drishaig *Strath*	E3	17
Drongan *Strath*	B4	12
Druimarbin *Highl*	A3	22
Druimavuic *Strath*	D1	17
Druimdhu *Highl*	A3	30
Drumbain *Highl*	D4	31
Drumbeg *Highl*	B3	36
Drumbuie *Highl*	D4	29
Drumburn *D. & G.*	F3	7
Drumchardine *Highl*	C3	30
Drumclog *Strath*	C3	12
Drumelzier *Borders*	F3	13
Drumgask *Highl*	D2	23
Drumguish *Highl*	E2	23
Drumin Castle *Grampn*	A4	32
Drumjohn *D. & G.*	D1	7
Drumlemble *Strath*	D4	11
Drummond *Highl*	C2	30
Drummore *D. & G.*	B4	6
Drummuir Castle *Grampn*	B3	32
Drumnadrochit *Highl*	C4	30
Drumnagorrach *Grampn*	C3	32
Drumoak *Grampn*	D2	25
Drumochter Lodge *Highl*	D3	23
Drumshang *Strath*	A4	12
Drumsturdy *Tays*	E1	19
Drumvaich *Central*	A3	18
Drybridge *Strath*	B3	12
Drymen *Central*	F4	17
Drymuir *Grampn*	E3	33
Drynoch *Highl*	B4	28
Dubford *Grampn*	D2	33
Duchally *Highl*	D4	37
Duddo *Northum*	D2	15
Dudley *T. & W.*	F2	9
Dufftown *Grampn*	B3	32
Duffus *Grampn*	A2	32
Duible *Highl*	F4	37

Duirinish *Highl*	D4	29
Duisdalemore *Highl*	E1	21
Duisky *Highl*	A3	22
Dull *Tays*	B1	18
Dulnain Bridge *Highl*	E4	31
Dulsie *Highl*	E3	31
Dumbarton *Strath*	B1	12
Dumeath *Grampn*	B4	32
Dumfries *D. & G.*	F2	7
Dumgoyne *Central*	A4	18
Dunan *Highl*	C4	28
Dunan *Strath*	A1	12
Dunan *Tays*	C4	22
Dunbar *Lothn*	F4	19
Dunbeath *Highl*	B3	38
Dunbeg *Strath*	C1	16
Dunblane *Central*	B3	18
Duncanston *Highl*	C3	30
Dundee *Tays*	E2	19
Dundonald *Strath*	B3	12
Dundonnell *Highl*	F1	29
Dundreggan *Highl*	B1	22
Dundrennan *D. & G.*	E3	7
Dunduff *Fife*	C3	18
Dunecht *Grampn*	D1	25
Dunfermline *Fife*	C4	18
Dunino *Fife*	E3	19
Dunipace *Central*	B4	18
Dunkeld *Tays*	C1	18
Dunlappie *Tays*	C3	24
Dunlop *Strath*	B2	12
Dunmore *Strath*	E2	11
Dunnet *Highl*	B1	38
Dunning *Tays*	C2	18
Dunoon *Strath*	E4	17
Dunragit *D. & G.*	B3	6
Dunrostan *Strath*	C4	16
Duns *Borders*	C2	14
Dunscore *D. & G.*	E2	7
Dunshelt *Fife*	D3	19
Dunshillock *Grampn*	E3	33
Duntocher *Strath*	C1	12
Duntulm *Highl*	B2	28
Dunure *Strath*	A4	12
Dunvegan *Highl*	B3	28
Durham *Durham*	F4	9
Durisdeermill *D. & G.*	F1	7
Durness *Highl*	D1	37
Durran *Highl*	B2	38
Dury *Shetld*	C3	40
Duthil *Highl*	E4	31
Dyce *Grampn*	E1	25
Dykehead *Central*	A3	18
Dykehead *Tays*	B4	24
Dykends *Tays*	B4	24
Dysart *Fife*	D3	19
Eaglesfield *D. & G.*	A2	8
Eaglesham *Strath*	C2	12
Eamont Bridge *Cumbr*	C4	8
Earlish *Highl*	B2	28
Earlsferry *Fife*	E3	19
Earlston *Borders*	B3	14
Easdale *Strath*	C2	16
East Calder *Lothn*	E1	13
East Cramlington *Northum*	F2	9
East Croachy *Highl*	D4	31
East Darlochan *Strath*	D3	11
East Kilbride *Strath*	C2	12
East Langwell *Highl*	E4	37
East Linton *Lothn*	F4	19
East Ord *Northum*	D2	15
East Plean *Central*	B4	18
East Saltoun *Lothn*	B1	14
East Wemyss *Fife*	D3	19
Easter Balmoral *Grampn*	B2	24
Easter Fearn *Highl*	D1	31
Easter Kinkell *Highl*	C3	30
Easter Lednathie *Tays*	B4	24
Easter Quarff *Shetld*	B3	40
Eastertown *Grampn*	B4	32
Eastfield *Strath*	D1	13
Eastgate *Durham*	E4	9
Eastlands *D. & G.*	E2	7
Eastriggs *D. & G.*	A3	8
Ebchester *Durham*	F3	9
Ecclaw *Borders*	C1	14
Ecclefechan *D. & G.*	A2	8
Eccles *Borders*	C2	14
Ecclesmachan *Lothn*	E1	13
Echt *Grampn*	D2	25
Edderton *Highl*	D1	31
Eddleston *Borders*	F2	13
Edinburgh *Lothn*	F1	13
Edingham *D. & G.*	E3	7
Edmondbyers *Durham*	E3	9
Ednam *Borders*	C3	14
Edzell *Tays*	C3	24
Effirth *Shetld*	B3	40
Eglingham *Northum*	E4	15
Eilanreach *Highl*	E1	21
Eileanach Lodge *Highl*	C2	30
Eldrick *Strath*	C2	6
Elgin *Grampn*	B2	32
Elgol *Highl*	D1	21
Elie *Fife*	E3	19
Elishaw *Northum*	D1	9
Ellemford Bridge *Borders*	C2	14
Ellington *Northum*	F1	9
Ellon *Grampn*	E4	33
Elphin *Highl*	C4	36
Elsdon *Northum*	E1	9
Elsrickle *Strath*	E2	13
Elvanfoot *Strath*	E4	13
Embleton *Cumbr*	A4	8
Embleton *Northum*	F3	15
Enoch *D. & G.*	F1	7
Enochdhu *Tays*	F4	23
Ensay *Strath*	A1	16
Enterkinfoot *D. & G.*	E1	7
Eoligarry *W. Isles*	E3	27
Eoropie *W. Isles*	E1	35
Erchless Castle *Highl*	B3	30
Eredine *Strath*	D3	17
Eriboll *Highl*	D2	37
Erines *Strath*	E1	11
Errogie *Highl*	C4	30
Errol *Tays*	D2	19
Ervie *D. & G.*	A2	6
Esh Winning *Durham*	F4	9
Eskbank *Lothn*	A1	14
Eskdalemuir *D. & G.*	A1	8
Etal *Northum*	D3	15
Ettrick *Borders*	A4	14
Ettrickbridge *Borders*	B3	14
Evanton *Highl*	C2	30
Evelix *Highl*	D1	31
Evertown *D. & G.*	B2	8
Eyemouth *Borders*	D1	15
Eyre *Highl*	B3	28
Failford *Strath*	B3	12
Fairlie *Strath*	A2	12
Fala *Lothn*	B2	14
Falkirk *Central*	B4	18
Falkland *Fife*	D3	19
Fallford *D. & G.*	B2	8
Fallin *Central*	B3	18
Fanagmore *Highl*	C2	36
Fanmore *Strath*	A1	16
Fannich Lodge *Highl*	B2	30
Farmtown *Grampn*	C3	32
Farr *Highl*	E2	37
Fasnakyle *Highl*	B4	30
Fauldhouse *Lothn*	E2	13
Fearn *Highl*	E2	31
Fearn Lodge *Highl*	C1	30
Fearnan *Tays*	A1	18
Fearnmore *Highl*	D3	29
Felling *T. & W.*	F3	9
Felton *Northum*	F1	9
Fenwick *Northum*	E3	15
Fenwick *Strath*	B2	12
Feochaig *Strath*	D4	11
Feolin Ferry *Strath*	C1	10
Fern *Tays*	C4	24
Ferness *Highl*	E3	31
Fernie *Fife*	D2	19
Fernilea *Highl*	B4	28
Ferryhill *Durham*	F4	9
Feshiebridge *Highl*	E2	23
Fettercairn *Grampn*	D3	25
Fiag Bridge *Highl*	D4	37
Fiag Lodge *Highl*	D3	37
Fiddes *Grampn*	D3	25
Finavon *Tays*	C4	24
Fincharn *Strath*	D3	17
Findhorn *Grampn*	E2	31
Findochty *Grampn*	C2	32
Findon Mains *Highl*	C2	30
Fingland *Cumbr*	A3	8
Finnart *Tays*	C4	22
Finnygaud *Grampn*	C3	32
Finstown *Orkney*	B3	39
Fintry *Central*	A4	18
Fintry *Grampn*	D3	33
Fionnphort *Strath*	A2	16
Fir Tree *Durham*	F4	9
Fisherford *Grampn*	D4	33
Fisherton *Strath*	B4	12
Fishwick *Borders*	D2	15
Fiskavaig *Highl*	B4	28
Fiunary *Highl*	B1	16
Five Penny Borve *W. Isles*	D1	35
Five Penny Ness *W. Isles*	E1	35
Flashader *Highl*	B3	28
Flimby *Cumbr*	F4	7
Flodden *Northum*	D3	15
Flodigarry *Highl*	C2	28
Flosh *D. & G.*	A2	8
Flotterton *Northum*	E1	9
Flushing *Grampn*	E3	33
Fochabers *Grampn*	B3	32
Fodderletter *Grampn*	A4	32
Fogorig *Borders*	C2	14
Foindle *Highl*	C2	36
Ford *Northum*	D3	15
Ford *Strath*	C3	16
Fordoun *Grampn*	D3	25
Forest *Durham*	D4	9
Forest Lodge *Strath*	E1	17
Forest Mill *Central*	C3	18
Forestburn Gate *Northum*	E1	9
Forfar *Tays*	C4	24
Forgie *Grampn*	B3	32
Forres *Grampn*	E3	31
Forrestfield *Strath*	D1	13
Forsinard *Highl*	F2	37
Fort Augustus *Highl*	C1	22
Fort George *Highl*	D3	31
Fort William *Highl*	A3	22
Forteviot *Tays*	C2	18
Forth *Strath*	E2	13
Fortingall *Tays*	B1	18
Fortrie *Grampn*	D3	33
Fortrose *Highl*	D3	31
Fothergill *Cumbr*	F4	7
Foulden *Borders*	D2	15
Fourstones *Northum*	D2	9
Foveran *Grampn*	E4	33
Fowlis Wester *Tays*	B2	18
Foyers *Highl*	C1	22
Fraserburgh *Grampn*	E2	33
Freswick *Highl*	C1	38
Freuchie *Fife*	D3	19
Friarton *Tays*	C2	18
Friockheim *Tays*	F1	19
Frogden *Borders*	C3	14
Frosterley *Durham*	E4	9
Fullarton *Strath*	B3	12
Funzie *Shetld*	C2	40
Furnace *Strath*	D3	17
Fyvie *Grampn*	D4	33
Gaick Lodge *Highl*	E3	23
Gairloch *Highl*	D2	29
Gairlochy *Highl*	B3	22
Gairney Bank *Tays*	C3	18
Gairnshiel Lodge *Grampn*	B2	24
Galashiels *Borders*	B3	14
Gallanach *Strath*	B4	20
Gallanach *Strath*	C2	16
Gallatown *Fife*	D3	19
Gallowfauld *Tays*	E1	19
Galltair *Highl*	E1	21
Galmisdale *Highl*	D3	21
Galston *Strath*	C3	12
Gamblesby *Cumbr*	C4	8
Gannochy *Tays*	C3	24
Garbat *Highl*	B2	30
Garbhallt *Strath*	D3	17
Garchory *Grampn*	B1	24
Gardenstown *Grampn*	D2	33
Garderhouse *Shetld*	B3	40
Garelochhead *Strath*	E3	17
Garlieston *D. & G.*	D3	7
Garlogie *Grampn*	D2	25
Garmony *Strath*	B1	16
Garmouth *Grampn*	B2	32
Garrabost *W. Isles*	E2	35
Garrick *Tays*	B3	18
Garrow *Tays*	B1	18
Gartachoil *Central*	A3	18
Gartcosh *Strath*	D1	13
Gartly *Grampn*	C4	32
Gartnagrenach *Strath*	E2	11
Gartocharn *Strath*	F4	17
Garvald *Borders*	A2	14
Garvan *Highl*	F3	21
Garve *Highl*	B2	30
Garvie *Strath*	D4	17
Garvock *Strath*	A1	12
Garynahine *W. Isles*	D2	35
Gass *Strath*	B4	12
Gasstown *D. & G.*	F2	7
Gatehead *Strath*	B3	12
Gatehouse of Fleet *D. & G.*	D3	7
Gateshaw *Borders*	C3	14
Gateshead *T. & W.*	F3	9
Gateside *Fife*	D3	19
Gateside *Strath*	B2	12
Gateside *Tays*	E1	19
Gavinton *Borders*	C2	14
Gayfield *Orkney*	B1	39
Geary *Highl*	B2	28
Gedintailor *Highl*	C4	28
Gelston *D. & G.*	E3	7
Georth *Orkney*	B2	39
Geshader *W. Isles*	C2	34
Gibbshill *D. & G.*	E2	7

Gifford *Lothn*	B1	14
Gillfoot *D. & G.*	F2	7
Gillock *Highl*	B2	38
Gillroanie *D. & G.*	E3	7
Gills *Highl*	C1	38
Gilmanscleuch *Borders*	A3	14
Gilmerton *Tays*	B2	18
Gilsland *Northum*	C3	8
Girlsta *Shetld*	B3	40
Girvan *Strath*	B1	6
Gisla *W. Isles*	C2	34
Glackour *Highl*	A1	30
Gladsmuir *Lothn*	B1	14
Glame *Highl*	C3	28
Glamis *Tays*	E1	19
Glancaple *D. & G.*	F2	7
Glanton *Northum*	E4	15
Glasgow *Strath*	C1	12
Glasnacardoch *Highl*	E2	21
Glassburn *Highl*	B4	30
Glasserton *D. & G.*	C4	6
Glebe *Highl*	C1	22
Glemanuilt *Strath*	D4	11
Glenbarr *Strath*	D3	11
Glenbeg *Highl*	D4	21
Glenboig *Strath*	D1	13
Glenborrodale *Highl*	D4	21
Glenbranter *Strath*	E3	17
Glenbreck *Borders*	E3	13
Glenbrittle *Highl*	C1	20
Glencarron Lodge *Highl*	F3	29
Glencarse *Tays*	D2	19
Glencassley Castle *Highl*	D4	37
Glencoe *Highl*	A4	22
Glencraig *Fife*	D3	19
Glendevon *Tays*	C3	18
Glendoebeg *Highl*	C1	22
Glendoick *Tays*	D2	19
Glenelg *Highl*	E1	21
Glenfarg *Tays*	C3	18
Glenfeshie Lodge *Highl*	E2	23
Glenfinnan *Highl*	F3	21
Glenfintaig *Highl*	B3	22
Glengarnock *Strath*	B2	12
Glengoulandie *Tays*	E4	23
Glengrasco *Highl*	C3	28
Glenkerry *Borders*	A4	14
Glenkindie *Grampn*	C1	24
Glenleraig *Highl*	C3	36
Glenlochar *D. & G.*	E3	7
Glenloig *Strath*	E3	11
Glenluce *D. & G.*	B3	6
Glenochar *Strath*	E4	13
Glenprosen Village *Tays*	B4	24
Glenrisdell *Strath*	E2	11
Glenrothes *Fife*	D3	19
Glentrool Village *D. & G.*	C2	6
Glenurquhart *Highl*	D2	31
Glenvarragill *Highl*	C3	28
Glespin *Strath*	D3	13
Glororum *Northum*	E3	15
Gloup *Shetld*	C1	40
Glutt Lodge *Highl*	A3	38
Gobernuisgach Lodge *Highl*	D3	37
Gogar *Lothn*	F1	13
Golden Fleece *Cumbr*	B3	8
Golspie *Highl*	D1	31
Golval *Highl*	F2	37
Gordon *Borders*	C2	14
Gordonbush *Highl*	F4	37
Gordonstown *Grampn*	C3	32
Gorebridge *Lothn*	A2	14
Gorrenberry *Borders*	B1	8
Gorstan *Highl*	B2	30
Gosforth *T. & W.*	F2	9
Gourock *Strath*	E4	17
Grandtully *Tays*	E4	23
Grangemouth *Central*	B4	18
Granton *Lothn*	F1	13
Grantown-on-Spey *Highl*	E4	31
Grantshouse *Borders*	D1	15
Graven *Shetld*	B2	40
Gravir *W. Isles*	D3	35
Great Clifton *Cumbr*	F4	7
Great Salkeld *Cumbr*	C4	8
Greendykes *Northum*	E3	15
Greengairs *Strath*	D1	13
Greenhead *Northum*	C3	8
Greenhill *Tays*	C3	18
Greenlaw *Borders*	C2	14
Greenlaw *Grampn*	D3	33
Greenloaning *Tays*	B3	18
Greenock *Strath*	E4	17
Greenside *T. & W.*	F3	9
Grenetote *W. Isles*	B2	26
Gress *W. Isles*	E2	35
Gretna *D. & G.*	B3	8
Gretna Green *D. & G.*	B2	8
Greystoke *Cumbr*	B4	8
Griminish *W. Isles*	C2	26
Grimister *Shetld*	C1	40
Grimmet *Strath*	B4	12
Grimshader *W. Isles*	D2	35
Grishipoll *Strath*	B4	20
Gritley *Orkney*	B3	39
Grogport *Strath*	E2	11
Grudie *Highl*	B2	30
Gruids *Highl*	E4	37
Gruinard House *Highl*	E1	29
Gruline *Strath*	B1	16
Grumbeg *Highl*	E3	37
Grutness *Shetld*	B4	40
Gualachulain *Strath*	E1	17
Gualin House *Highl*	C2	36
Guardbridge *Fife*	E2	19
Guay *Tays*	C1	18
Guide Post *Northum*	F2	9
Guildtown *Tays*	C2	18
Gullane *Lothn*	E4	19
Gutcher *Shetld*	C1	40
Habost *W. Isles*	D3	35
Haddington *Lothn*	B1	14
Halkirk *Highl*	B2	38
Hall *Strath*	B2	12
Hallbankgate *Cumbr*	C3	8
Hallin *Highl*	B3	28
Hallyne *Borders*	F3	13
Halmyre Mains *Borders*	F2	13
Halton Lea Gate *Northum*	C3	8
Haltwhistle *Northum*	D3	9
Ham *Shetld*	A3	40
Hamilton *Strath*	D2	13
Hamnavoe *Shetld*	B3	40
Hamnavoe *Shetld*	C2	40
Hamnavoe *Shetld*	C2	40
Hamsterley *Durham*	F3	9
Happendon *Strath*	D3	13
Harbottle *Northum*	D4	15
Hardgate *Grampn*	C4	32
Harelawhill *D. & G.*	B2	8
Harker *Cumbr*	B3	8
Harlow Hill *Northum*	E2	9
Haroldswick *Shetld*	C1	40
Harrapool *Highl*	D4	29
Harrietfield *Tays*	C2	18
Harrietsfield *Borders*	C3	14
Harris *Highl*	C2	20
Hartburn *Northum*	E2	9
Harthill *Strath*	E1	13
Hartside *Strath*	E3	13
Harvieston *Highl*	F3	37
Hassendean *Borders*	B3	14
Hastigrow *Highl*	B2	38
Hatton of Fintray *Grampn*	D1	25
Haugh Head *Northum*	D3	15
Haugh of Glass *Grampn*	B4	32
Haugh of Urr *D. & G.*	E3	7
Haughend *Tays*	C3	24
Hawick *Borders*	B4	14
Hawkhill *Northum*	F4	15
Hawksdale *Cumbr*	B3	8
Haydon Bridge *Northum*	D3	9
Hayhillock *Tays*	E1	19
Hazelbank *Strath*	D2	13
Heast *Highl*	D1	21
Hebburn *T. & W.*	F3	9
Heddon-on-the-Wall *Northum*	F3	9
Heilam *Highl*	D2	37
Heiton *Borders*	C3	14
Helensburgh *Strath*	E4	17
Helmsdale *Highl*	A4	38
Hempriggs *Grampn*	F2	31
Heogan *Shetld*	C3	40
Hepple *Northum*	E1	9
Heriot *Borders*	B2	14
Hermitage *Borders*	C1	8
Herston *Orkney*	B4	39
Hesleyside *Northum*	D2	9
Heugh *Northum*	E2	9
Hexham *Northum*	E3	9
Hexpath *Borders*	C2	14
High Bankhill *Cumbr*	C4	8
High Blantyre *Strath*	C2	12
High Etherley *Durham*	F4	9
High Glenling *D. & G.*	C3	6
High Harrington *Cumbr*	F4	7
High Hesket *Cumbr*	B4	8
High Lorton *Cumbr*	A4	8
High Scales *Cumbr*	A4	8
High Spen *T. & W.*	F3	9
Higham Dykes *Northum*	F2	9
Highchesters *Borders*	B4	14
Highfield *Strath*	B2	12
Hill End *Fife*	C3	18
Hill Head *Northum*	E2	9
Hill of Fearn *Highl*	D2	31
Hillend *Fife*	D4	19
Hillend *Shetld*	C2	40
Hillside *Shetld*	B2	40
Hillside *Tays*	D4	25
Hillswick *Shetld*	B2	40
Hilton *Grampn*	E4	33
Holland *Orkney*	C2	39
Hollandstoun *Orkney*	C1	39
Hollee *D. & G.*	B2	8
Hollows *D. & G.*	B2	8
Hollybush *Strath*	B4	12
Holmhead *Strath*	C3	12
Holy Island *Northum*	E2	15
Holystone *Northum*	E1	9
Holytown *Strath*	D2	13
Holywood *D. & G.*	F2	7
Hope *Highl*	D2	37
Hopeman *Grampn*	A2	32
Horsley *Northum*	D1	9
Horsley *Northum*	F3	9
Horsleyhill *Borders*	B4	14
Hougharry *W. Isles*	B3	26
Houndslow *Borders*	C2	14
Houndwood *Borders*	D1	15
Housetter *Shetld*	B2	40
Housieside *Grampn*	E4	33
Houston *Strath*	B1	12
Hoversta *Shetld*	C3	40
Howden le Wear *Durham*	F4	9
Howford *Borders*	A3	14
Howgate *Lothn*	F2	13
Howmore *W. Isles*	D3	27
Hownam *Borders*	C4	14
Howtel *Northum*	D3	15
Howwood *Strath*	B2	12
Huna *Highl*	C1	38
Hunspow *Highl*	B1	38
Hunters Quay *Strath*	E4	17
Huntford *Borders*	C4	14
Hunthill Lodge *Tays*	C3	24
Huntingtower *Tays*	C2	18
Huntly *Grampn*	C3	32
Huntlywood *Borders*	C2	14
Hunwick *Durham*	F4	9
Hurlford *Strath*	B3	12
Husinish *W. Isles*	B3	34
Huxter *Shetld*	C3	40
Hyndford Bridge *Strath*	E2	13
Hynish *Strath*	A1	20
Idrigill *Highl*	B2	28
Imachar *Strath*	E3	11
Inchbae Lodge *Highl*	B2	30
Inchbare *Tays*	C3	24
Inchberry *Grampn*	B3	32
Incheoch *Tays*	B4	24
Inchlaggan *Highl*	B2	22
Inchnacardoch *Highl*	C1	22
Inchnadamph *Highl*	C3	36
Innellan *Strath*	A1	12
Innerleithen *Borders*	A3	14
Innermessan *D. & G.*	B3	6
Innerwick *Tays*	D4	23
Insch *Grampn*	C4	32
Insh *Highl*	E2	23
Inshaig *Highl*	F4	21
Inver *Grampn*	B2	24
Inver *Highl*	E1	31
Inver *Tays*	C1	18
Inverailort *Highl*	E3	21
Inverallochy *Grampn*	E2	33
Inveraray *Strath*	D3	17
Inverarish *Highl*	C4	28
Inverarnan *Strath*	F2	17
Inverasdale *Highl*	D1	29
Inverbeg *Strath*	F3	17
Inverbervie *Grampn*	D3	25
Invercharnan *Strath*	E1	17
Inverdruie *Highl*	E1	23
Inveresk *Lothn*	A1	14
Inveresragan *Strath*	D1	17
Inverewe House *Highl*	E2	29
Inverey *Grampn*	F2	23
Inverfarigaig *Highl*	C4	30
Invergarry *Highl*	B2	22
Invergeldie *Tays*	B2	18
Invergloy *Highl*	B2	22
Invergordon *Highl*	D2	31
Invergowrie *Tays*	D2	19
Inverhadden *Tays*	D4	23
Inverherive *Strath*	F2	17
Inverinan *Strath*	D2	17
Inverinate *Highl*	E4	29
Inverkeilor *Tays*	F1	19
Inverkeithing *Fife*	C4	18
Inverkip *Strath*	A1	12
Inverlochlarig *Central*	F2	17
Invermark Lodge *Tays*	C3	24
Invermoriston *Highl*	C1	22
Invermossat *Grampn*	C1	24
Inverness *Highl*	D3	31

Inveroran Hotel *Strath* — E1 17
Inverpattack Lodge *Highl* — D2 23
Inversanda *Highl* — F4 21
Invershin *Highl* — C1 30
Inversnaid *Central* — F3 17
Inveruglas *Strath* — F3 17
Inverurie *Grampn* — D1 25
Invervar *Tays* — A1 18
Ireshopeburn *Durham* — D4 9
Irvine *Strath* — B3 12
Isauld *Highl* — A1 38
Isbister *Shetld* — B2 40
Isle of Whithorn *D. & G.* — D4 7
Islesteps *D. & G.* — F2 7
Jackton *Strath* — C2 12
Jamestown *Strath* — F4 17
Janetstown *Highl* — C2 38
Jawcraig *Central* — D1 13
Jedburgh *Borders* — C3 14
Jemimaville *Highl* — D2 31
Jessiefield *Grampn* — E2 25
John o'Groats *Highl* — C1 38
Johnshaven *Grampn* — D3 25
Johnstone *D. & G.* — A1 8
Johnstone *Strath* — B1 12
Johnstonebridge *D. & G.* — A1 8
Juniper Green *Lothn* — F1 13
Kaimes *Lothn* — A1 14
Kalemouth *Borders* — C3 14
Kames *Strath* — F1 11
Keig *Grampn* — C1 24
Keil *Highl* — F4 21
Keilhill *Grampn* — D3 33
Keillmore *Strath* — C4 16
Keiss *Highl* — C2 38
Keith *Grampn* — C3 32
Kellan *Strath* — B1 16
Kellas *Tays* — E1 19
Kellas *Grampn* — A3 32
Kelso *Borders* — C3 14
Keltneyburn *Tays* — B1 18
Kelty *Fife* — D3 19
Kemnay *Grampn* — D1 25
Kempie *Highl* — D2 37
Kenmore *Tays* — B1 18
Kennacley *W. Isles* — C4 34
Kennet *Central* — B3 18
Kennethmont *Grampn* — C4 32
Kennoway *Fife* — D3 19
Kensaleyre *Highl* — C3 28
Kentallen *Highl* — A4 22
Kenton Bankfoot *T. & W.* — F2 9
Kentra *Highl* — D3 21
Keoldale *Highl* — D1 37
Keppoch *Highl* — E4 29
Kerrycroy *Strath* — F2 11
Kerrysdale *Highl* — D2 29
Kershader *W. Isles* — D3 35
Kettlebridge *Fife* — D3 19
Kettleholm *D. & G.* — A2 8
Kettletoft *Orkney* — C2 39
Kielder *Northum* — C1 8
Kiells *Strath* — C1 10
Kilberry *Strath* — D1 11
Kilbirnie *Strath* — B2 12
Kilbride *Strath* — C2 16
Kilbride *W. Isles* — E3 27
Kilchattan *Strath* — A3 16
Kilchattan *Strath* — F2 11
Kilchenzie *Strath* — D3 11
Kilcheran *Strath* — C1 16
Kilchiaran *Strath* — B2 10
Kilchoan *Highl* — D4 21
Kilchrenan *Strath* — D2 17
Kilconquhar *Fife* — E3 19
Kilcreggan *Strath* — E4 17
Kildalloig *Strath* — D4 11
Kildavanan *Strath* — F1 11
Kildermorie Lodge *Highl* — C2 30
Kildonan *Highl* — F4 37
Kildrummy *Grampn* — C1 24
Kilfinan *Strath* — D4 17
Killchianaig *Strath* — B4 16
Killean *Strath* — D2 11
Killearn *Central* — A4 18
Killichonan *Tays* — D4 23
Killiechronan *Strath* — B1 16
Killiecrankie *Tays* — E4 23
Killilan *Highl* — E4 29
Killimster *Highl* — C2 38
Killin *Central* — A2 18
Killochyett *Borders* — B2 14
Killundine *Highl* — B1 16
Kilmacolm *Strath* — B1 12
Kilmahog *Central* — A3 18
Kilmalieu *Highl* — F4 21
Kilmaluag *Highl* — C2 28
Kilmany *Fife* — E2 19
Kilmarie *Highl* — D1 21

Kilmarnock *Strath* — B3 12
Kilmartin *Strath* — C3 16
Kilmaurs *Strath* — B2 12
Kilmelford *Strath* — C2 16
Kilmichael *Strath* — D3 11
Kilmorack *Highl* — C3 30
Kilmore *Highl* — D2 21
Kilmore *Strath* — C2 16
Kilmory *Highl* — C2 20
Kilmory *Strath* — D1 11
Kilmote *Highl* — A4 38
Kilmuir *Highl* — B3 28
Kilmun *Strath* — E4 17
Kilncadzow *Strath* — D2 13
Kilninian *Strath* — A1 16
Kilninver *Strath* — C2 16
Kilnpit Hill *Northum* — E3 9
Kiloran *Strath* — A3 16
Kilpatrick *Strath* — E3 11
Kilphedir *Highl* — A4 38
Kilsyth *Strath* — A4 18
Kilvaxter *Highl* — B2 28
Kilwinning *Strath* — B2 12
Kinbrace *Highl* — F3 37
Kinbuck *Central* — B3 18
Kincardine *Fife* — C4 18
Kincardine *Highl* — C1 30
Kincardine O'Neil *Grampn* — C2 24
Kincraig *Highl* — E2 23
Kindallachan *Tays* — F4 23
Kingarth *Strath* — F2 11
Kinghorn *Fife* — D4 19
Kinglassie *Fife* — D3 19
Kingoodie *Grampn* — D1 25
Kingoodie *Tays* — D2 19
Kingsbarns *Fife* — F3 19
Kingseat *Fife* — C4 18
Kingsford *Strath* — B2 12
Kingshouse *Central* — A2 18
Kingskettle *Fife* — D3 19
Kingsmuir *Fife* — E3 19
Kingsmuir *Tays* — E1 19
Kingston *Grampn* — B2 32
Kingston *Lothn* — E4 19
Kingstown *Cumbr* — B3 8
Kingswells *Grampn* — E2 25
Kingussie *Highl* — D2 23
Kinkell Bridge *Tays* — B2 18
Kinloch *Highl* — D3 37
Kinloch *Tays* — D1 19
Kinloch Castle *Highl* — C2 20
Kinloch Hourn *Highl* — F2 21
Kinloch Lodge *Highl* — D2 37
Kinloch Rannoch *Tays* — D4 23
Kinlochard *Central* — F3 17
Kinlochbervie *Highl* — C2 36
Kinlocheil *Highl* — F3 21
Kinlochewe *Highl* — E2 29
Kinlochleven *Highl* — B4 22
Kinlochspelve *Highl* — B2 16
Kinloss *Grampn* — F2 31
Kinmundy *Grampn* — E1 25
Kinnesswood *Tays* — D3 19
Kinross *Tays* — C3 18
Kintaravay *W. Isles* — D3 35
Kintocher *Grampn* — C1 24
Kintore *Grampn* — D1 25
Kintour *Strath* — C2 10
Kintraw *Strath* — C3 16
Kinveachy *Highl* — E1 23
Kippen *Central* — A3 18
Kirivick *W. Isles* — C2 34
Kirk Merrington *Durham* — F4 9
Kirk *Highl* — B2 38
Kirkabister *Shetld* — C3 40
Kirkbampton *Cumbr* — B3 8
Kirkbride *Cumbr* — A3 8
Kirkby Thore *Cumbr* — C4 8
Kirkcaldy *Fife* — D3 19
Kirkcambeck *Cumbr* — C2 8
Kirkcolm *D. & G.* — A2 6
Kirkconnel *D. & G.* — D4 13
Kirkcowan *D. & G.* — C3 6
Kirkcudbright *D. & G.* — E3 7
Kirkdale *D. & G.* — D3 7
Kirkdean *Borders* — F2 13
Kirkhill *Highl* — C3 30
Kirkhope *Borders* — B3 14
Kirkhouse *Borders* — A3 14
Kirkiboll *Highl* — E2 37
Kirkinner *D. & G.* — C3 6
Kirkintilloch *Strath* — C1 12
Kirkland *D. & G.* — E1 7
Kirkmaiden *D. & G.* — B4 6
Kirkmichael *Strath* — B4 12
Kirkmuirhill *Strath* — D2 13
Kirknewton *Northum* — D3 15
Kirkoswald *Cumbr* — C4 8
Kirkoswald *Strath* — A4 12

Kirkpatrick-Fleming *D. & G.* — B2 8
Kirkstile *D. & G.* — B1 8
Kirkton *Borders* — B4 14
Kirkton *Highl* — D1 31
Kirkton *Highl* — E3 29
Kirkton *Strath* — E3 13
Kirkton of Culsalmond *Grampn* — D4 33
Kirkton of Durris *Grampn* — D2 25
Kirkton of Kingoldrum *Tays* — B4 24
Kirkton of Largo *Fife* — E3 19
Kirkton of Lethendy *Tays* — C1 18
Kirkton of Menmuir *Tays* — C4 24
Kirkton of Oyne *Grampn* — D1 25
Kirkton of Skene *Grampn* — D1 25
Kirktown of Auchterless *Grampn* — D3 33
Kirktown of Deskford *Grampn* — C2 32
Kirkwall *Orkney* — B3 39
Kirn *Strath* — E4 17
Kirriemuir *Tays* — B4 24
Kirtlebridge *D. & G.* — A2 8
Kirtomy *Highl* — E2 37
Knarsdale *Northum* — C3 8
Knock *Strath* — B1 16
Knock *W. Isles* — E2 35
Knockan *Strath* — C4 36
Knockan *Strath* — A2 16
Knockandhu *Grampn* — A4 32
Knockban *Highl* — B3 30
Knockdolian Castle *Strath* — B2 6
Knockenkelly *Strath* — F3 11
Knockentiber *Strath* — B3 12
Knockglass *Highl* — A2 38
Knocklae *D. & G.* — D2 7
Knockycoid *Strath* — C2 6
Knowe *D. & G.* — C2 6
Knowehead *D. & G.* — D1 7
Knowesgate *Northum* — E2 9
Knowside *Strath* — A4 12
Kyle of Lochalsh *Highl* — D4 29
Kyleakin *Highl* — D4 29
Kylerhea *Highl* — E1 21
Kyles Scalpay *W. Isles* — D4 35
Kylestrome *Highl* — C3 36
Ladybank *Fife* — D3 19
Ladysford *Grampn* — E3 33
Lagavulin *Strath* — C2 10
Lagg *Strath* — B4 16
Lagg *Strath* — E3 11
Laggan *Grampn* — B4 32
Laggan *Highl* — B2 22
Laggan *Highl* — D2 23
Lagganbane *Highl* — B1 22
Lagganulva *Strath* — A1 16
Laide *Highl* — E1 29
Laigh Fenwick *Strath* — B2 12
Lair *Highl* — E3 29
Lairg *Highl* — E4 37
Lairgmore *Highl* — C4 30
Laithes *Cumbr* — B4 8
Lamberton *Borders* — D2 15
Lambley *Northum* — C3 8
Lamington *Strath* — E3 13
Lamlash *Strath* — F3 11
Lanark *Strath* — D2 13
Lanchester *Durham* — F3 9
Lane Ends *Durham* — F4 9
Lanehead *Durham* — D4 9
Langbank *Strath* — B1 12
Langburnshiels *Borders* — B4 14
Langdon Beck *Durham* — D4 9
Langholm *D. & G.* — B2 8
Langley *Northum* — D3 9
Langshaw *Borders* — B3 14
Langside *Tays* — B2 18
Langwathby *Cumbr* — C4 8
Larachbeg *Highl* — C1 16
Largiemore *Strath* — D4 17
Largoward *Fife* — E3 19
Largs *Strath* — A2 12
Largymore *Strath* — F3 11
Larkhall *Strath* — D2 13
Lasswade *Lothn* — A1 14
Latheron *Highl* — B3 38
Lathones *Fife* — E3 19
Lauder *Borders* — B2 14
Laurencekirk *Grampn* — D3 25
Laurieston *D. & G.* — E3 7
Law *Strath* — D2 13
Lawers *Tays* — A1 18
Laxay *W. Isles* — D3 35
Laxdale *W. Isles* — D2 35
Laxford Bridge *Highl* — C2 36
Laxo *Shetld* — C2 40
Lazonby *Cumbr* — C4 8
Leadburn *Lothn* — F2 13
Leaderfoot *Borders* — B3 14
Leadgate *Durham* — F3 9

Leadhills *Strath*	D4	13
Leanach *Strath*	D3	17
Leanaig *Highl*	C3	30
Leargybreck *Strath*	C1	10
Leaths *D. & G.*	E3	7
Leckfurin *Highl*	E2	37
Leckgruinart *Strath*	B1	10
Leckmelm *Highl*	A1	30
Ledaig *Strath*	D1	17
Ledcharrie *Central*	F2	17
Ledgowan *Highl*	A3	30
Ledmore *Highl*	C4	36
Leirinmore *Highl*	D1	37
Leith *Lothn*	A1	14
Leitholm *Borders*	C2	14
Lemreway *W. Isles*	D3	35
Lendalfoot *Strath*	B1	6
Lennel *Borders*	D3	15
Lennoxtown *Strath*	A4	18
Lenzie *Strath*	C1	12
Lephin *Highl*	A3	28
Lephinmore *Strath*	D3	17
Lerwick *Shetld*	C3	40
Lesbury *Northum*	F4	15
Leslie *Fife*	D3	19
Lesmahagow *Strath*	D3	13
Leswalt *D. & G.*	A3	6
Letterfearn *Highl*	E4	29
Letterfinlay *Highl*	B2	22
Letters *Highl*	A1	30
Lettershaws *Strath*	D3	13
Lettoch *Highl*	F4	31
Leuchars *Fife*	E2	19
Leurbost *W. Isles*	D2	35
Leven *Fife*	E3	19
Levenwick *Shetld*	B4	40
Leverburgh *W. Isles*	C4	34
Lewiston *Highl*	C4	30
Leylodge *Grampn*	D1	25
Lhanbryde *Grampn*	B2	32
Liatrie *Highl*	B4	30
Libberton *Strath*	E2	13
Liberton *Lothn*	A1	14
Liddesdale *Highl*	E4	21
Lilliesleaf *Borders*	B3	14
Limekilnburn *Strath*	D2	13
Limerigg *Central*	D1	13
Lindores *Fife*	D2	19
Linicro *Highl*	B2	28
Linktown *Fife*	D4	19
Linlithgow *Lothn*	E1	13
Linsidemore *Highl*	C1	30
Lintmill *Grampn*	C2	32
Linton *Borders*	C3	14
Linwood *Strath*	B1	12
Lionel *W. Isles*	E1	35
Little Assynt *Highl*	C3	36
Little Bavington *Northum*	E2	9
Little Creich *Highl*	D1	31
Little Dunkeld *Tays*	C1	18
Little Gruinard *Highl*	E1	29
Little Scatwell *Highl*	B3	30
Little Sypland *D. & G.*	E3	7
Little Torhouse *D. & G.*	C3	6
Littleferry *Highl*	D1	31
Littlemill *Grampn*	B2	24
Littlemill *Highl*	D4	31
Littlemill *Highl*	E3	31
Littlemill *Strath*	B4	12
Livingston *Lothn*	E1	13
Loanhead *Lothn*	A1	14
Loanhead *Strath*	E3	13
Loans *Strath*	B3	12
Loansdean *Northum*	F2	9
Loch Choire Lodge *Highl*	E3	37
Loch Loyal Lodge *Highl*	E2	37
Lochailort *Highl*	E3	21
Lochaline *Highl*	C1	16
Lochans *D. & G.*	B3	6
Locharbriggs *D. & G.*	F2	7
Lochassynt Lodge *Highl*	C3	36
Lochavich *Strath*	D2	17
Lochawe *Strath*	E2	17
Lochboisdale *W. Isles*	D2	27
Lochbuie *Highl*	B2	16
Lochcarron *Highl*	E3	29
Lochdonhead *Strath*	C1	16
Lochdrum *Highl*	B2	30
Lochead *Strath*	C4	16
Lochearnhead *Central*	A2	18
Lochend *Highl*	C4	30
Locheport *W. Isles*	B2	26
Locherben *D. & G.*	F1	7
Lochgair *Strath*	D4	17
Lochgarthside *Highl*	C1	22
Lochgelly *Fife*	D3	19
Lochgilphead *Strath*	C4	16
Lochgoilhead *Strath*	E3	17
Lochhead *Grampn*	C2	24
Lochhill *Strath*	C4	12
Lochinver *Highl*	B3	36
Lochluichart Lodge *Highl*	B2	30
Lochmaben *D. & G.*	A2	8
Lochmaddy *W. Isles*	B2	26
Lochore *Fife*	D3	19
Lochportain *W. Isles*	B2	26
Lochranza *Strath*	E2	11
Lochside *Highl*	F3	37
Lochuisge *Highl*	E4	21
Lochwinnoch *Strath*	B2	12
Lochy Bridge *Highl*	B3	22
Lockerbie *D. & G.*	A2	8
Logierait *Tays*	E4	23
Londubh *Highl*	E2	29
Longbenton *T. & W.*	F2	9
Longcastle *D. & G.*	C3	6
Longforgan *Tays*	D2	19
Longformacus *Borders*	C2	14
Longframlington *Northum*	F1	9
Longhirst *Northum*	F1	9
Longhope *Orkney*	A4	39
Longhorsley *Northum*	F1	9
Longhoughton *Northum*	F4	15
Longmanhill *Grampn*	D2	33
Longniddry *Lothn*	B1	14
Longridge *Lothn*	E2	13
Longside *Grampn*	E3	33
Longtown *Cumbr*	B2	8
Lonmore *Highl*	B3	28
Lootcherbrae *Grampn*	C3	32
Lorbottle *Northum*	E4	15
Lossiemouth *Grampn*	B2	32
Lothbeg *Highl*	A4	38
Lothmore *Highl*	A4	38
Low Brunton *Northum*	E2	9
Low Crosby *Cumbr*	B3	8
Low Gate *Northum*	E3	9
Low Hesket *Cumbr*	B3	8
Low Lorton *Cumbr*	A4	8
Lower Diabaig *Highl*	D3	29
Lower Killeyan *Strath*	B2	10
Lower Largo *Fife*	E3	19
Lower Milovaig *Highl*	A3	28
Lower Shader *W. Isles*	D1	35
Lowick *Northum*	E3	15
Lubcroy *Highl*	B1	30
Lubmore *Highl*	F3	29
Luffness *Lothn*	E4	19
Lugton *Strath*	B2	12
Luib *Highl*	C4	28
Lumphanan *Grampn*	C2	24
Lumsden *Grampn*	C4	32
Luncarty *Tays*	C2	18
Lundie *Highl*	B1	22
Lundin Links *Fife*	E3	19
Luskentyre *W. Isles*	C4	34
Luss *Strath*	F3	17
Lusta *Highl*	B3	28
Lybster *Highl*	B3	38
Lynchat *Highl*	E2	23
Lyne of Skene *Grampn*	D1	25
Lyneholmeford *Cumbr*	C2	8
Lynemouth *Northum*	F1	9
Lyness *Orkney*	A3	39
Lyth *Highl*	B2	38
Macduff *Grampn*	D2	33
Macharioch *Strath*	D4	11
Machrihanish *Strath*	D3	11
Macmerry *Lothn*	B1	14
Maddiston *Central*	E1	13
Maggieknockater *Grampn*	B3	32
Maiden Law *Durham*	F3	9
Maidens *Strath*	A4	12
Mains of Cairnborrow *Grampn*	C3	32
Mains of Craigmill *Grampn*	F3	31
Mains of Dalvey *Highl*	F4	31
Mains of Drum *Grampn*	D2	25
Mains of Dun *Tays*	D4	25
Mains of Glenbuchat *Grampn*	B1	24
Mains of Idoch *Grampn*	D3	33
Mains of Towie *Grampn*	D3	33
Mains of Watten *Highl*	B2	38
Mainsriddle *D. & G.*	F3	7
Mallaig *Highl*	E2	21
Maneight *Strath*	C4	12
Mangaster *Shetld*	B2	40
March *Strath*	E4	13
Marchburn *D. & G.*	C4	12
Margnaheglish *Strath*	F3	11
Marjoriebanks *D. & G.*	A2	8
Mark *Strath*	B2	6
Markinch *Fife*	D3	19
Marley Hill *T. & W.*	F3	9
Marnoch *Grampn*	C3	32
Maryburgh *Highl*	C3	30
Marygold *Borders*	D2	15
Maryhill *Strath*	C1	12
Marykirk *Grampn*	D3	25
Marypark *Grampn*	A4	32
Maryport *Cumbr*	F4	7
Maryton *Tays*	D4	25
Marywell *Tays*	F1	19
Marywell *Grampn*	C2	24
Mauchline *Strath*	C3	12
Maud *Grampn*	E3	33
Mawbray *Cumbr*	A3	8
Maxton *Borders*	C3	14
Maxwellston *Strath*	C1	6
Maybole *Strath*	B4	12
Mealsgate *Cumbr*	A4	8
Meavag *W. Isles*	C4	35
Medomsley *Durham*	F3	9
Meigle *Tays*	D1	19
Meikle Carco *D. & G.*	D4	13
Meikleour *Tays*	D1	19
Meikleyard *Strath*	C3	12
Melbourne *Strath*	E2	13
Melfort *Strath*	C2	16
Melgarve *Highl*	C2	22
Melkridge *Northum*	D3	9
Melldalloch *Strath*	E1	11
Mellon Charles *Highl*	E1	29
Mellon Udrigle *Highl*	E1	29
Melmerby *Cumbr*	C4	8
Melness *Highl*	E2	37
Melrose *Borders*	B3	14
Melvaig *Highl*	D1	29
Melvich *Highl*	F2	37
Memsie *Grampn*	E2	33
Mennock *D. & G.*	D4	13
Menstrie *Central*	B3	18
Merkadale *Highl*	B4	28
Merkland Lodge *Highl*	D3	37
Metal Bridge *Cumbr*	B3	8
Methil *Fife*	E3	19
Methlick *Grampn*	E4	33
Methven *Tays*	C2	18
Mey *Highl*	C1	38
Miavaig *W. Isles*	C2	34
Mickley Square *Northum*	E3	9
Mid Ardlaw *Grampn*	E2	33
Mid Beltie *Grampn*	C2	24
Mid Calder *Lothn*	E1	13
Mid Sannox *Strath*	F2	11
Mid Setter *Shetld*	B3	40
Midbea *Orkney*	B2	39
Middlebie *D. & G.*	A2	8
Middleshaw *D. & G.*	A2	8
Middlestone *Durham*	F4	9
Middleton *Northum*	E3	15
Middleton *Strath*	A1	20
Middleton in Teesdale *Durham*	E4	9
Midfield *Highl*	E1	37
Midgeholme *Cumbr*	C3	8
Midlem *Borders*	B3	14
Midtown *Highl*	E2	37
Midtown Brae *Highl*	D1	29
Milfield *Northum*	D3	15
Mill of Uras *Grampn*	E3	25
Millbounds *Orkney*	B2	39
Millbreck *Grampn*	E3	33
Millden Lodge *Tays*	C3	24
Milldens *Tays*	C4	24
Millerhill *Lothn*	A1	14
Millgrip *Orkney*	C2	39
Millheugh *Strath*	D2	13
Millhouse *Strath*	E1	11
Millikenpark *Strath*	B2	12
Millport *Strath*	A2	12
Milltimber *Grampn*	E2	25
Milton *Tays*	E1	19
Milton of Noth *Grampn*	C4	32
Milltown *Grampn*	C1	24
Milltown *Grampn*	C3	32
Milltown *Highl*	B3	30
Milltown of Aberdalgie *Tays*	C2	18
Milltown of Auchindoun *Grampn*	B3	32
Milltown of Campfield *Grampn*	D2	25
Milnacraig *Tays*	B4	24
Milnathort *Tays*	C3	18
Milngavie *Strath*	C1	12
Milton *Central*	F3	17
Milton *Central*	F4	17
Milton *Cumbr*	C3	8
Milton *Highl*	C4	30
Milton *Highl*	D2	31
Milton *Tays*	A4	24
Milton *Tays*	B1	18
Milton of Auchriachan *Grampn*	A1	24
Milton of Campsie *Strath*	C1	12
Milton of Cushnie *Grampn*	C1	24
Miltonish *D. & G.*	B2	6
Minard *Strath*	D3	17

Place	Region	Ref	Pg
Mindrum	Northum	D3	15
Mindrummill	Northum	D3	15
Minishant	Strath	B4	12
Mintlaw	Grampn	E3	33
Mitford	Northum	F2	9
Modsarie	Highl	E2	37
Moffat	D. & G.	E4	13
Monevechadan	Strath	E3	17
Moniaive	D. & G.	E1	7
Monifieth	Tays	E2	19
Monkton	Strath	B3	12
Monreith	D. & G.	C4	6
Montgreenan	Strath	B2	12
Montrose	Tays	D4	25
Monymusk	Grampn	D1	25
Moor of Granary	Grampn	F3	31
Moorhouse	Cumbr	B3	8
Morar	Highl	E2	21
Morebattle	Borders	C3	14
Morefield	Highl	F1	29
Morenish	Tays	A1	18
Morpeth	Northum	F2	9
Morvich Lodge	Highl	D1	31
Moscow	Strath	C3	12
Moss Side	Cumbr	A3	8
Mossat	Grampn	C1	24
Mossbank	Shetld	C2	40
Mossdale	D. & G.	D2	7
Mossdale	Strath	C4	12
Mossend	Strath	D2	13
Mosspaul Hotel	Borders	B1	8
Mosstodloch	Grampn	B3	32
Motherby	Cumbr	B4	8
Motherwell	Strath	D2	13
Moulin	Tays	E4	23
Moulinearn	Tays	F4	23
Mount Pleasant	Borders	C2	14
Mountain Cross	Borders	F2	13
Mountbenger	Borders	A3	14
Mouswald	D. & G.	F2	7
Moy	Highl	C3	22
Moy	Highl	D4	31
Moy Lodge	Highl	C3	22
Muasdale	Strath	D3	11
Muchalls	Grampn	E2	25
Mudale	Highl	D3	37
Muie	Highl	E4	37
Muir	Grampn	F2	23
Muir of Fowlis	Grampn	C1	24
Muir of Ord	Highl	C3	30
Muirdrum	Tays	E1	19
Muirhead	Fife	D3	19
Muirhead	Strath	C1	12
Muirhead	Tays	D1	19
Muirkirk	Strath	C3	12
Muirshearlich	Highl	B3	22
Muirton of Ardblair	Tays	D1	19
Mulben	Grampn	B3	32
Munerigie	Highl	B2	22
Mungasdale	Highl	E1	29
Munlochy	Highl	D3	31
Murkle	Highl	B1	38
Murlaggan	Highl	A2	22
Murthly	Tays	C1	18
Musselburgh	Lothn	A1	14
Mutehill	D. & G.	E3	7
Muthill	Tays	B2	18
Mybster	Highl	B2	38
Nairn	Highl	E3	31
Naust	Highl	D1	29
Navidale	Highl	A4	38
Nedd	Highl	C3	36
Neilston	Strath	B2	12
Nenthall	Cumbr	D4	9
Nenthead	Cumbr	D4	9
Nenthorn	Borders	C3	14
Nerston	Strath	C2	12
Ness	Orkney	B2	39
Nether Dalgliesh	Borders	A4	14
Nether Whitecleuch	Strath	D3	13
Netherley	Grampn	E2	25
Netherthird	Strath	C4	12
Netherton	Central	A4	18
Netherton	Tays	C4	24
Nethy Bridge	Highl	F1	23
Nettlesworth	Durham	F3	9
New Abbey	D. & G.	F3	7
New Aberdour	Grampn	E2	33
New Alyth	Tays	D1	19
New Bewick	Northum	E3	15
New Byth	Grampn	D3	33
New Cumnock	Strath	C4	12
New Deer	Grampn	E3	33
New Delaval	Northum	F2	9
New Galloway	D. & G.	D2	7
New Kelso	Highl	E3	29
New Leeds	Grampn	E3	33
New Luce	D. & G.	B3	6
New Mains of Ury	Grampn	E2	25
New Monkland	Strath	D1	13
New Pitsligo	Grampn	E3	33
New Sauchie	Central	B3	18
New Scone	Tays	C2	18
New Tolsta	W. Isles	E1	35
New Town	Lothn	B1	14
Newbiggin	Cumbr	C3	8
Newbiggin	Durham	E4	9
Newbiggin-by-the-Sea	Northum	F2	9
Newbigging	Borders	B2	14
Newbigging	Strath	E2	13
Newbigging	Tays	B3	24
Newbigging	Tays	E1	19
Newburgh	Borders	A4	14
Newburgh	Fife	D2	19
Newburgh	Grampn	E1	25
Newby Cross	Cumbr	B3	8
Newcastle-upon-Tyne	T. & W.	F3	9
Newcastleton	Borders	C2	8
Newfield	D. & G.	E3	7
Newhall	Borders	A3	14
Newhouse	Strath	D2	13
Newkirk	Grampn	C2	24
Newlands	Borders	C1	8
Newlands	Grampn	B3	32
Newlands	Northum	E3	9
Newmachar	Grampn	E1	25
Newmains	Strath	D2	13
Newmarket	W. Isles	D2	35
Newmill	Borders	B4	14
Newmill	Grampn	C3	32
Newmilns	Strath	C3	12
Newport	Highl	B3	38
Newport-on-Tay	Fife	E2	19
Newtack	Grampn	C3	32
Newton	Borders	C3	14
Newton	D. & G.	B2	8
Newton	Grampn	C3	32
Newton	Grampn	C4	32
Newton	Highl	C3	30
Newton	Highl	D2	31
Newton	Highl	D3	31
Newton	Lothn	C4	18
Newton	Tays	B2	18
Newton Arlosh	Cumbr	A3	8
Newton Mearns	Strath	C2	12
Newton Reigny	Cumbr	C4	8
Newton Stewart	D. & G.	C3	6
Newtongarry Croft	Grampn	C4	32
Newtongrange	Lothn	A1	14
Newtonhill	Grampn	E2	25
Newtonmore	Highl	D2	23
Newtown	Cumbr	C3	8
Newtown	Grampn	A2	32
Newtown St. Boswells	Borders	B3	14
Newtyle	Tays	D1	19
Nickie's Hill	Cumbr	C2	8
Nigg	Grampn	E2	25
Nigg	Highl	D2	31
Nigg Ferry	Highl	D2	31
Ninemile Bar or Crocketford	D. & G.	E2	7
Nisbet	Borders	C3	14
Norham	Northum	D2	15
North Ballachulish	Highl	A4	22
North Balloch	Strath	C1	6
North Berwick	Lothn	E4	19
North Boisdale	W. Isles	D3	27
North Charlton	Northum	E3	15
North Craigo	Tays	D4	25
North Craigs	D. & G.	B2	8
North Erradale	Highl	D2	29
North Greenhill	Cumbr	C2	8
North Kessock	Highl	D3	31
North Middleton	Lothn	A2	14
North Port	Strath	D2	17
North Queensferry	Fife	C4	19
North Sandwick	Shetld	C1	40
North Togston	Northum	F1	9
North Tolsta	W. Isles	E1	35
North Water Bridge	Tays	D3	25
Northmuir	Tays	B4	24
Northton	W. Isles	B4	34
Norwick	Shetld	C1	40
Nostie	Highl	E4	29
Nybster	Highl	C1	38
Oakwood	Borders	B3	14
Oban	Strath	C2	16
Ochiltree	Strath	C3	12
Ochtermuthill	Tays	B2	18
Ockle	Highl	D3	21
Old Bridge of Urr	D. & G.	E2	7
Old Dailly	Strath	B1	6
Old Deer	Grampn	E3	33
Old Hall House	Highl	B2	38
Old Howford	Borders	A3	14
Old Kilpatrick	Strath	B1	12
Old Scone	Tays	C2	18
Oldany	Highl	B3	36
Oldmeldrum	Grampn	D1	25
Oldshore	Highl	C2	36
Olgrinmore	Highl	B2	38
Ollaberry	Shetld	B2	40
Ollach	Highl	C4	28
Onich	Highl	A4	22
Opinan	Highl	D2	29
Opinan	Highl	E1	29
Orange Lane	Borders	C2	14
Ord	Highl	D1	21
Ordens	Grampn	C2	32
Ordhead	Grampn	D1	25
Ordie	Grampn	C2	24
Orgill	Orkney	A3	39
Ormiscaig	Highl	E1	29
Ormiston	Lothn	B1	14
Ornsay	Highl	E1	21
Oskamull	Strath	A1	16
Osnaburgh or Dairsie	Fife	E2	19
Otter Ferry	Strath	D4	17
Otterburn	Northum	D1	9
Otterswick	Shetld	C2	40
Ousby	Cumbr	C4	8
Outchester	Northum	E3	15
Overscaig House	Highl	D3	37
Overtown	Strath	D2	13
Oxnam	Borders	C4	14
Oxton	Borders	B2	14
Oykel Bridge	Highl	B1	30
Oyne	Grampn	D1	25
Padanaram	Tays	B4	24
Paddockhole	D. & G.	A2	8
Paisley	Strath	B1	12
Palnackie	D. & G.	E3	7
Palnure	D. & G.	C3	6
Park	D. & G.	F1	7
Park	Strath	D1	17
Park End	Northum	D2	9
Parkdargue	Grampn	C3	32
Parkend	Cumbr	B4	8
Parkgate	Cumbr	A3	8
Parkgate	D. & G.	F1	7
Parsonby	Cumbr	A4	8
Partick	Strath	C1	12
Parton	D. & G.	E2	7
Pathead	Strath	C4	12
Pathhead	Grampn	D4	25
Pathhead	Lothn	B1	14
Patna	Strath	B4	12
Pauperhaugh	Northum	E1	9
Paxton	Borders	D2	15
Pearsie	Tays	B4	24
Peat Inn	Fife	E3	19
Peatknowe	Grampn	C3	32
Peebles	Borders	A3	14
Pegswood	Northum	F2	9
Peinchorran	Highl	C4	28
Peinmore	Highl	C3	28
Pelton	Durham	F3	9
Pelutho	Cumbr	A3	8
Pencaitland	Lothn	B1	14
Penicuik	Lothn	F2	13
Peninver	Strath	D3	11
Penkill	Strath	B1	6
Pennan	Grampn	D2	33
Pennyghael	Strath	B2	16
Pennyglen	Strath	A4	12
Pennygown	Strath	B1	16
Pennyvenie	Strath	C4	12
Penpont	D. & G.	E1	7
Penrith	Cumbr	C4	8
Penruddock	Cumbr	B4	8
Perceton	Strath	B3	12
Percyhorner	Grampn	E2	33
Perth	Tays	C2	18
Peterburn	Highl	D1	29
Peterculter	Grampn	D2	25
Peterhead	Grampn	F3	33
Petterden	Tays	E1	19
Pettymuick	Grampn	E1	25
Philiphaugh	Borders	B3	14
Pierowall	Orkney	B1	39
Pinminnoch	Strath	B1	6
Pinmore	Strath	B1	6
Pinwherry	Strath	B2	6
Pirnmill	Strath	E2	11
Pitcaple	Grampn	D1	25
Pitchroy	Grampn	A4	32
Pitcox	Lothn	C1	14
Pitcur	Tays	D1	19
Pitlessie	Fife	D3	19
Pitlochry	Tays	E4	23
Pitmachie	Grampn	D4	33
Pitmedden	Grampn	E1	25
Pitscottie	Fife	E2	19
Pittendreich	Grampn	A2	32

Pittentrail *Highl*	D1	31
Pittenweem *Fife*	F3	19
Plaidy *Grampn*	D3	33
Plains *Strath*	D1	13
Plean *Central*	B4	18
Plockton *Highl*	D4	29
Plumpton Head *Cumbr*	C4	8
Polbain *Highl*	B4	36
Polbeth *Lothn*	E1	13
Polloch *Highl*	E3	21
Pollokshaws *Strath*	C2	12
Polmaddie *D. & G.*	D2	7
Polmoody *D. & G.*	F4	13
Polnessan *Strath*	B4	12
Polwarth *Borders*	C2	14
Ponteland *Northum*	F2	9
Pool of Muckart *Central*	C3	18
Poolewe *Highl*	E2	29
Porin *Highl*	B3	30
Port Appin *Strath*	D1	17
Port Askaig *Strath*	C1	10
Port Bannatyne *Strath*	F1	11
Port Charlotte *Strath*	B2	10
Port Driseach *Strath*	F1	11
Port Ellen *Strath*	C2	10
Port Elphinstone *Grampn*	D1	25
Port Glasgow *Strath*	B1	12
Port Henderson *Highl*	D2	29
Port Lamont *Strath*	F1	11
Port Logan *D. & G.*	B4	6
Port na Long *Highl*	B4	28
Port nan Long *W. Isles*	B2	26
Port of Menteith *Central*	A3	18
Port of Ness *W. Isles*	E1	35
Port Ramsay *Strath*	C1	16
Port Seton *Lothn*	B1	14
Port Wemyss *Strath*	B2	10
Port William *D. & G.*	C4	6
Portencross *Strath*	A2	12
Portessie *Grampn*	C2	32
Portgordon *Grampn*	B2	32
Portgower *Highl*	A4	38
Portincaple *Strath*	E3	17
Portinnisherrich *Strath*	D3	17
Portknockie *Grampn*	C2	32
Portlethen *Grampn*	E2	25
Portmahomack *Highl*	E1	31
Portnacroish *Highl*	D1	17
Portnaguiran *W. Isles*	E2	35
Portnahaven *Strath*	B2	10
Portnaluchaig *Highl*	D2	21
Portnancon *Highl*	D2	37
Portnellan *Central*	F2	17
Portobello *Lothn*	A1	14
Portpatrick *D. & G.*	A3	6
Portree *Highl*	C3	28
Portskerra *Highl*	F1	37
Portslogan *D. & G.*	A3	6
Portsonachan *Strath*	D2	17
Portsoy *Grampn*	C2	32
Poundland *Strath*	B2	6
Powburn *Northum*	E4	15
Powmill *Tays*	C3	18
Preston *Borders*	C2	14
Preston *Lothn*	F4	19
Prestonmill *D. & G.*	F3	7
Prestonpans *Lothn*	B1	14
Prestwick *Strath*	B3	12
Primrosehill *Borders*	C2	14
Prior Muir *Fife*	E2	19
Protstonhill *Grampn*	D2	33
Prudhoe *Northum*	E3	9
Pulcree *D. & G.*	D3	7
Pumpherston *Lothn*	E1	13
Purvishaugh *Borders*	C3	14
Queensferry *Lothn*	C4	18
Queenzieburn *Strath*	A4	18
Quoig *Tays*	B2	18
Quoyburray *Orkney*	B3	39
Rackwick *Orkney*	A3	39
Rackwick *Orkney*	B1	39
Radernie *Fife*	E3	19
Raerinish *W. Isles*	D3	35
Rafford *Grampn*	F3	31
Raise *Cumbr*	D3	9
Ranfurly *Strath*	B1	12
Rannoch Station *Tays*	C4	22
Ranochan *Highl*	E3	21
Rapness *Orkney*	B2	39
Rashiereive *Grampn*	E1	25
Rathillet *Fife*	E2	19
Ratho *Lothn*	F1	13
Rattar *Highl*	B1	38
Ratten Row *Cumbr*	B4	8
Rattray *Tays*	D1	19
Ravenstruther *Strath*	E2	13
Raylees *Northum*	E1	9
Reay *Highl*	A1	38
Red Dial *Cumbr*	B4	8
Red Row *Northum*	F1	9
Redburn *Highl*	C2	30
Redburn *Highl*	E3	31
Redford *Tays*	F1	19
Redmyre *Grampn*	D3	25
Redpoint *Highl*	D2	29
Rehourie *Highl*	E3	31
Reiff *Highl*	B4	36
Reisque *Grampn*	E1	25
Reiss *Highl*	C2	38
Relugas *Grampn*	E3	31
Remony *Tays*	B1	18
Renfrew *Strath*	C1	12
Rennington *Northum*	E4	15
Renton *Strath*	F4	17
Renwick *Cumbr*	C4	8
Rescobie *Tays*	C4	24
Resolis *Highl*	D2	31
Rest and be Thankful *Strath*	E3	17
Reston *Borders*	D2	15
Rhemore *Highl*	D4	21
Rhian *Highl*	E4	37
Rhicarn *Highl*	B3	36
Rhiconich *Highl*	C2	36
Rhiedorrach *Tays*	A3	24
Rhilochan *Highl*	E4	37
Rhiroy *Highl*	A1	30
Rhu *Strath*	E4	17
Rhunahaorine *Strath*	D2	11
Rhynie *Grampn*	C4	32
Riccarton *Strath*	B3	12
Rickarton *Grampn*	D2	25
Ridsdale *Northum*	E2	9
Rig *D. & G.*	D4	13
Rigg *D. & G.*	B3	8
Riggend *Strath*	D1	13
Rigside *Strath*	D3	13
Ringford *D. & G.*	E3	7
Roadhead *Cumbr*	C2	8
Roadside *Highl*	B2	38
Roadside *Orkney*	C2	39
Roadside of Kinneff *Grampn*	D3	25
Roan of Craigoch *Strath*	C1	6
Roberton *Borders*	B4	14
Roberton *Strath*	E3	13
Rochester *Northum*	D1	9
Rodel *W. Isles*	C4	34
Rogart *Highl*	E4	37
Romannobridge *Borders*	F2	13
Rootpark *Strath*	E2	13
Rosehall *Highl*	C1	30
Rosehearty *Grampn*	E2	33
Rosemarkie *Highl*	D3	31
Rosemount *Tays*	D1	19
Rosewell *Lothn*	A2	14
Roshven *Highl*	E3	21
Roskhill *Highl*	B3	28
Rosley *Cumbr*	B4	8
Rosneath *Strath*	E4	17
Roster *Highl*	B3	38
Rosyth *Fife*	C4	18
Rothbury *Northum*	E1	9
Rothes *Grampn*	B3	32
Rothesay *Strath*	F1	11
Rothienorman *Grampn*	D4	33
Rottal *Tays*	B3	24
Roughburn *Highl*	C3	22
Roughsike *Cumbr*	C2	8
Roundstonefoot *D. & G.*	F4	13
Rovie Lodge *Highl*	E4	37
Rowland's Gill *T. & W.*	F3	9
Rowley *Durham*	E3	9
Rowmore *Strath*	E4	17
Roybridge *Highl*	B3	22
Ruaig *Strath*	A1	20
Ruffside *Durham*	E3	9
Runtaleave *Tays*	B3	24
Rushyford *Durham*	F4	9
Ruskie *Central*	A3	18
Rutherglen *Strath*	C1	12
Ruthven *Highl*	E2	23
Ruthven *Tays*	D1	19
Ryton *T. & W.*	F3	9
Sacriston *Durham*	F3	9
Saddell *Strath*	E3	11
St. Abbs *Borders*	D1	15
St. Andrews *Fife*	E2	19
St. Ann's *D. & G.*	F1	7
St. Boswells *Borders*	C3	14
St. Catherines *Strath*	E3	17
St. Colmac *Strath*	F1	11
St. Combs *Grampn*	E2	33
St. Cyrus *Grampn*	D3	25
St. Fergus *Grampn*	F3	33
St. Fillans *Tays*	A2	18
St. Helen Auckland *Durham*	F4	9
St. John's Chapel *Durham*	E4	9
St. John's Town of Dalry *D. & G.*	D2	7
St. Katherines *Grampn*	D4	33
St. Madoes *Tays*	D2	19
St. Margaret's Hope *Orkney*	B3	39
St. Mary's *Orkney*	B3	39
St. Monans *Fife*	E3	19
St. Ninians *Central*	B3	18
St. Quivox *Strath*	B3	12
Salen *Highl*	E3	21
Salen *Strath*	B1	16
Saline *Fife*	C3	18
Sallachy *Highl*	D4	37
Sallachy *Highl*	E4	29
Salsburgh *Strath*	D2	13
Saltcoats *Strath*	A3	12
Saltness *Orkney*	A4	39
Samsonlane *Orkney*	C2	39
Sanachan *Highl*	E3	29
Sanaigmore *Strath*	B1	10
Sandbank *Strath*	E4	17
Sandgarth *Orkney*	B3	39
Sandhaven *Grampn*	E2	33
Sandhead *D. & G.*	B3	6
Sandholm *Borders*	C1	8
Sandness *Shetld*	B3	40
Sandquoy *Orkney*	C2	39
Sandwick *W. Isles*	E2	35
Sandyford *D. & G.*	A1	8
Sandyford *Strath*	B3	12
Sangobeg *Highl*	D1	37
Sanquhar *D. & G.*	D4	13
Satley *Durham*	F4	9
Sauchieburn *Grampn*	D3	25
Saughtree *Borders*	C1	8
Savary *Highl*	B1	16
Scadabay *W. Isles*	C4	34
Scalasaig *Strath*	A3	16
Scalloway *Shetld*	B3	40
Scar *Orkney*	C2	39
Scarastavore *W. Isles*	C4	34
Scardroy *Highl*	B3	30
Scarfskerry *Highl*	B1	38
Scarinish *Strath*	A1	20
Scarwell *Orkney*	A2	39
Sconser *Highl*	C4	28
Scots Gap *Northum*	E2	9
Scotsdike *Cumbr*	B2	8
Scotston *Grampn*	D3	25
Scotston *Tays*	B1	18
Scotstown *Highl*	E4	21
Scourie *Highl*	C3	36
Scousburgh *Shetld*	B4	40
Scrabster *Highl*	B1	38
Scremerston *Northum*	D2	15
Scriberscross *Highl*	F4	37
Seafield *Highl*	C3	28
Seafield *Strath*	B3	12
Seahouses *Northum*	E3	15
Seamill *Strath*	A2	12
Seaton Burn *T. & W.*	F2	9
Seaton Delaval *Northum*	F2	9
Sebergham *Cumbr*	B4	8
Seghill *Northum*	F2	9
Selkirk *Borders*	B3	14
Setter *Shetld*	C2	40
Shandford *Tays*	C4	24
Shandon *Strath*	E4	17
Shannochie *Strath*	F3	11
Shawbost *W. Isles*	D2	35
Shawhead *D. & G.*	E2	7
Shearington *D. & G.*	F3	7
Shebster *Highl*	A2	38
Sheigra *Highl*	C2	36
Sheillahill *D. & G.*	E3	7
Shennanton *D. & G.*	C3	6
Shenval *Grampn*	A4	32
Shiel Bridge *Highl*	F1	21
Shieldaig *Highl*	D3	29
Shieldaig Lodge *Highl*	D2	29
Shieldhill *Central*	D1	13
Shildon *Durham*	F4	9
Shillmoor *Northum*	D4	15
Shiltenish *W. Isles*	D3	35
Shinness *Highl*	D4	37
Shiskine *Strath*	E3	11
Shore Mill *Highl*	D2	31
Shotley Bridge *Durham*	E3	9
Shulishader *W. Isles*	E2	35
Sibster *Highl*	C2	38
Siddick *Cumbr*	F4	7
Silloth *Cumbr*	A3	8
Silverford *Grampn*	D2	33
Simprim *Borders*	D2	15
Sinclairston *Strath*	B4	12
Sinderhope *Northum*	D3	9
Singdean *Borders*	C1	8
Skail *Highl*	E2	37
Skaill *Orkney*	B2	39
Skares *Grampn*	C4	32

Place	Ref	Page
Skares *Strath*	C4	12
Skateraw *Lothn*	C1	14
Skaw *Shetld*	C2	40
Skellister *Shetld*	C3	40
Skelmorlie *Strath*	A1	12
Skelton *Cumbr*	B4	8
Skerray *Highl*	E2	37
Skigersta *W. Isles*	E1	35
Skinidin *Highl*	B3	28
Skipness *Strath*	E2	11
Skirling *Borders*	E3	13
Skirwith *Cumbr*	C4	8
Slackhead *Grampn*	B2	32
Slaggyford *Northum*	C3	8
Slamannan *Central*	D1	13
Slattadale *Highl*	E2	29
Sleekburn *Northum*	F2	9
Slickly *Highl*	C1	38
Sliddery *Strath*	E3	11
Sligachan *Highl*	C4	28
Slochd *Highl*	E4	31
Slochnacraig *Tays*	A3	24
Slockavullin *Strath*	C3	16
Slumbay *Highl*	E4	29
Smailholm *Borders*	C3	14
Smallburn *Strath*	C3	12
Smithfield *Cumbr*	B3	8
Smithstown *Highl*	D2	29
Sorbie *D. & G.*	C3	6
Sorbietrees *Borders*	C2	8
Sordale *Highl*	B2	38
Sorisdale *Strath*	C4	20
Sorn *Strath*	C3	12
Sornhill *Strath*	C3	12
South Alloa *Central*	B3	18
South Ballachulish *Highl*	A4	22
South Broomhill *Northum*	F1	9
South Carrine *Strath*	D4	11
South Charlton *Northum*	E3	15
South Hourat *Strath*	B2	12
South Kirkton *Grampn*	D2	25
South Limmerhaugh *Strath*	C3	12
South Moor *Durham*	F3	9
Southdean *Borders*	C4	14
Southend *Strath*	D4	11
Soutra Mains *Lothn*	B2	14
Soval Lodge *W. Isles*	D3	35
Spartylea *Northum*	D3	9
Spean Bridge *Highl*	B3	22
Spennymoor *Durham*	F4	9
Spey Bay *Grampn*	B2	32
Speybridge *Highl*	E4	31
Speyview *Grampn*	B3	32
Spinningdale *Highl*	D1	31
Spittal *D. & G.*	C3	6
Spittal *Highl*	B2	38
Spittal *Lothn*	B1	14
Spittal of Glenmuick *Grampn*	B3	24
Spittal of Glenshee *Tays*	A3	24
Spittalfield *Tays*	C1	18
Springfield *Grampn*	E3	31
Springholm *D. & G.*	E2	7
Springwell *T. & W.*	F3	9
Sprouston *Borders*	C3	14
Sronphadruig Lodge *Tays*	D3	23
Staffin *Highl*	C2	28
Stainton *Cumbr*	C4	8
Stair *Strath*	B3	12
Stakeford *Northum*	F2	9
Stamfordham *Northum*	E2	9
Stand *Strath*	D1	13
Standburn *Central*	E1	13
Stane *Strath*	D2	13
Stanhope *Durham*	E4	9
Stanley *Durham*	F3	9
Stanley *Tays*	C2	18
Stannersburn *Northum*	D2	9
Stannington *Northum*	F2	9
Steele Road *Borders*	C1	8
Stenhousemuir *Central*	B4	18
Stenscoll *Highl*	C2	28
Stenton *Lothn*	C1	14
Stepps *Strath*	C1	12
Stevenston *Strath*	A2	12
Stewarton *Strath*	B2	12
Stewarton *Strath*	D4	11
Stichill *Borders*	C3	14
Stirling *Central*	B3	18
Stirling *Grampn*	F3	33
Stittenham *Highl*	D2	31
Stobo *Borders*	F3	13
Stockiemuir *Central*	F4	17
Stocksfield *Northum*	E3	9
Stoer *Highl*	B3	36
Stonehaven *Grampn*	E3	25
Stonehouse *Strath*	D2	13
Stoneybridge *W. Isles*	D3	27
Stoneyburn *Lothn*	E2	13
Stoneykirk *D. & G.*	B3	6
Stoneywood *Grampn*	E1	25
Stornoway *W. Isles*	D2	35
Stove *Shetld*	B4	40
Stow *Borders*	B2	14
Straad *Strath*	F2	11
Strachan *Grampn*	D2	25
Strachur *Strath*	E3	17
Straiton *Strath*	B4	12
Straloch *Tays*	F4	23
Stranraer *D. & G.*	B3	6
Strath *Highl*	B2	38
Strath Kanaird *Highl*	C4	36
Strathan *Highl*	F2	21
Strathaven *Strath*	D2	13
Strathblane *Central*	A4	18
Strathcarron *Highl*	E3	29
Strathcoil *Strath*	C2	16
Strathdon *Grampn*	B1	24
Strathmashie House *Highl*	D2	23
Strathmiglo *Fife*	D3	19
Strathmore Lodge *Highl*	B2	38
Strathpeffer *Highl*	C3	30
Strathtay *Tays*	E4	23
Strathwhillan *Strath*	F3	11
Strathy *Highl*	F1	37
Strathyre *Central*	A2	18
Strichen *Grampn*	E3	33
Stromeferry *Highl*	E4	29
Stromemore *Highl*	E4	29
Stromness *Orkney*	A3	39
Stronachlachar *Central*	F3	17
Stronchreggan *Highl*	A3	22
Strond *W. Isles*	C4	34
Strone *Highl*	B3	22
Strone *Highl*	C4	30
Strone *Strath*	E4	17
Stronenaba *Highl*	B3	22
Stronmilchan *Strath*	E2	17
Strontian *Highl*	E4	21
Struan *Highl*	B4	28
Struy *Highl*	B3	30
Stuartfield *Grampn*	E3	33
Studdon *Northum*	D3	9
Sullom *Shetld*	B2	40
Sunadale *Strath*	E2	11
Sunderland Bridge *Durham*	F4	9
Sunniside *Durham*	F4	9
Sunniside *T. & W.*	F3	9
Swanbister *Orkney*	A3	39
Swarland *Northum*	F1	9
Swiney *Highl*	B3	38
Swinnie *Borders*	C4	14
Swinton *Borders*	D2	15
Swintonmill *Borders*	D2	15
Symbister *Shetld*	C3	40
Syre *Highl*	E2	37
Tain *Highl*	D1	31
Tairlaw *Strath*	C1	6
Talla Linfoots *Borders*	F3	13
Talladale *Highl*	E2	29
Talmine *Highl*	E2	37
Talnotry *D. & G.*	D2	7
Tannadice *Tays*	C4	24
Tantobie *Durham*	F3	9
Tarbert *Strath*	D2	11
Tarbert *Strath*	E1	11
Tarbert *W. Isles*	C4	34
Tarbet *Highl*	C2	36
Tarbet *Strath*	F3	17
Tarbolton *Strath*	B3	12
Tarfside *Tays*	C3	24
Tarland *Grampn*	C2	24
Tarskavaig *Highl*	D1	21
Tarves *Grampn*	E3	33
Tayinloan *Strath*	D2	11
Taynuilt *Strath*	D2	17
Tayport *Fife*	E2	19
Tayvallich *Strath*	C4	16
Teangue *Highl*	D1	21
Temon *Cumbr*	C3	8
Templand *D. & G.*	A2	8
Temple Sowerby *Cumbr*	C4	8
Tepper Moor *Northum*	D2	9
Terally *D. & G.*	B4	6
Teviothead *Borders*	B4	14
Thirlestane *Borders*	B2	14
Thornhill *Central*	A3	18
Thornhill *D. & G.*	E1	7
Thornliebank *Strath*	C2	12
Thornthwaite *Cumbr*	A4	8
Thornton *Fife*	D3	19
Thorntonloch *Lothn*	C1	14
Throphill *Northum*	F2	9
Thropton *Northum*	E1	9
Thrumster *Highl*	C3	38
Thursby *Cumbr*	B3	8
Thurso *Highl*	B1	38
Thurstonfield *Cumbr*	B3	8
Tigerton *Tays*	C4	24
Tighnabruaich *Strath*	F1	11
Tillicoultry *Central*	B3	18
Tillyfourie *Grampn*	D1	25
Tinnis *Borders*	A3	14
Tirril *Cumbr*	C4	8
Tobermory *Strath*	D4	21
Toberonochy *Strath*	C3	16
Todhills *Cumbr*	B3	8
Toft Hill *Durham*	F4	9
Togston *Northum*	F1	9
Tokavaig *Highl*	D1	21
Toll of Birness *Grampn*	E4	33
Tomatin *Highl*	D4	31
Tombreck *Highl*	D4	31
Tomdoun *Highl*	B2	22
Tomich *Highl*	B4	30
Tomich *Highl*	C3	30
Tomintoul *Grampn*	A1	24
Tomnavoulin *Grampn*	A4	32
Tomphubil *Tays*	E4	23
Tong *W. Isles*	E2	35
Tongland *D. & G.*	E3	7
Tongue *Highl*	E2	37
Torbeg *Grampn*	B2	24
Torbeg *Strath*	E3	11
Tore *Highl*	C3	30
Torgyle Bridge *Highl*	B1	22
Torinturk *Strath*	E1	11
Torlundy *Highl*	B3	22
Tormore *Strath*	E3	11
Tornahaish *Grampn*	B1	24
Tornapress *Highl*	D3	29
Tornaveen *Grampn*	C2	24
Torness *Highl*	C4	30
Torosay Castle *Strath*	C1	16
Torphichen *Lothn*	E1	13
Torphins *Grampn*	C2	24
Torran *Strath*	C3	16
Torrance *Strath*	C1	12
Torrans *Strath*	B2	16
Torridon *Highl*	E3	29
Torrin *Highl*	D1	21
Torrisdale *Highl*	E2	37
Torrish *Highl*	A4	38
Torrlaoighseach *Highl*	F1	21
Torthorwald *D. & G.*	F2	7
Toscaig *Highl*	D4	29
Totaig *Highl*	E4	29
Totegan *Highl*	F1	37
Totscore *Highl*	B2	28
Tournaig *Highl*	E1	29
Tow Law *Durham*	F4	9
Toward *Strath*	A1	12
Towiemore *Grampn*	B3	32
Town Yetholm *Borders*	D3	15
Townhead of Greenlaw *D. & G.*	E3	7
Trabboch *Strath*	B3	12
Tranent *Lothn*	B1	14
Trantlemore *Highl*	F2	37
Traquair *Borders*	A3	14
Tresta *Shetld*	B3	40
Tresta *Shetld*	C2	40
Trinity *Tays*	C4	25
Trislaig *Highl*	A3	22
Trochry *Tays*	C1	18
Trondavoe *Shetld*	B2	40
Troon *Strath*	B3	12
Troutbeck *Cumbr*	B4	8
Trows *Borders*	C3	14
Tudhoe *Durham*	F4	9
Tullibody *Central*	B3	18
Tullich *Highl*	E2	31
Tullich *Highl*	D2	17
Tullochcan *Central*	A1	18
Tullochgorm *Strath*	D3	17
Tullynessle *Grampn*	C1	24
Tummel Bridge *Tays*	E4	23
Turnberry *Strath*	A4	12
Turriff *Grampn*	D3	33
Twechar *Strath*	C1	12
Tweedmouth *Northum*	D2	15
Tweedshaws *Borders*	E4	13
Twice Brewed *Northum*	D3	9
Twynholm *D. & G.*	D3	7
Tyndrum *Central*	F2	17
Tynehead *Lothn*	B2	14
Tyninghame *Fife*	F4	19
Tynribbie *Strath*	D1	17
Tynron *D. & G.*	E1	7
Uddingston *Strath*	D2	13
Uddington *Strath*	D3	13
Udstonhead *Strath*	D2	13
Ugadale *Strath*	E3	11
Uidh *W. Isles*	E3	27
Uig *Highl*	B2	28
Uig *Strath*	B4	20
Uig *Strath*	E4	17
Uig *W. Isles*	C2	34

Uisken *Strath*	A2	16
Ulbster *Highl*	C3	38
Ulgham *Northum*	F1	9
Ullapool *Highl*	F1	29
Ulsta *Shetld*	C2	40
Unapool *Highl*	C3	36
Under Burnmouth *Borders*	B2	8
Upper Ardchronie *Highl*	C1	30
Upper Coll *W. Isles*	E2	35
Upper Druimfin *Strath*	D4	21
Upper Knockando *Grampn*	A3	32
Upper Milovaig *Highl*	A3	28
Upper Mumbie *D. & G.*	B2	8
Upper Rusko *D. & G.*	D3	7
Upper Sandaig *Highl*	E1	21
Upper Scoulag *Strath*	F2	11
Upperby *Cumbr*	B3	8
Uppertown *Orkney*	B3	39
Urafirth *Shetld*	B2	40
Urray *Highl*	C3	30
Ushaw Moor *Durham*	F4	9
Usworth *T. & W.*	F3	9
Uyeasound *Shetld*	C1	40
Valleyfield *D. & G.*	E3	7
Valtos *Highl*	C2	28
Valtos *W. Isles*	C2	34
Veensgarth *Strath*	B3	40
Vidlin *Shetld*	C2	40
Voe *Shetld*	B2	40
Voensgarth *Shetld*	B3	40
Walker *T. & W.*	F3	9
Walkerburn *Borders*	A3	14
Wall *Northum*	E2	9
Wallaceton *D. & G.*	E2	7
Walls *Shetld*	B3	40
Wallsend *T. & W.*	F3	9
Wallyford *Lothn*	A1	14
Walton *Cumbr*	C3	8
Walton Park *D. & G.*	E2	7
Walwick *Northum*	E2	9
Wamphraygate *D. & G.*	A1	8
Wanlockhead *D. & G.*	D4	13
Waren Mill *Northum*	E3	15
Warenford *Northum*	E3	15
Wark *Northum*	D2	9
Wark *Northum*	D3	15
Warkworth *Northum*	F4	15
Warwick *Cumbr*	B3	8
Warwick Bridge *Cumbr*	C3	8
Wasbister *Orkney*	B2	39
Watchcross *Cumbr*	B3	8
Waterbeck *D. & G.*	A2	8
Waterfoot *Strath*	C2	12
Waterheads *Borders*	F2	13
Waterloo *Tays*	C1	18
Waterside *Strath*	B2	12
Waterside *Strath*	B4	12
Watten *Highl*	B2	38
Wattston *Strath*	D1	13
Waughslea *D. & G.*	B2	8
Waverbridge *Cumbr*	A3	8
Waverton *Cumbr*	A3	8
Wearhead *Durham*	D4	9
Wedderlairs *Grampn*	E4	33
Weisdale *Shetld*	B3	40
Weem *Tays*	B1	18
Weldon Bridge *Northum*	F1	9
Wellbank *Tays*	E1	19
Wellwood *Fife*	C4	18
Welton *Cumbr*	B4	8
Wemyss Bay *Strath*	A1	12
West Allerdean *Northum*	D2	15
West Auckland *Durham*	F4	9
West Barns *Lothn*	F4	19
West Belsay *Northum*	E2	9
West Calder *Lothn*	E1	13
West Cauldcoats *Strath*	C3	12
West Croachy *Highl*	D4	31
West Edington *Northum*	F2	9
West Geirinish *W. Isles*	C2	26
West Kilbride *Strath*	A2	12
West Kyloe *Northum*	E3	15
West Linton *Borders*	F2	13
West Mains *Northum*	E2	15
West Mains *Strath*	E2	13
West Moor *T. & W.*	F2	9
West Muir *Tays*	C4	24
West Nubbock *Northum*	E3	9
West Peaston *Lothn*	B1	14
West Pelton *Durham*	F3	9
West Sandwick *Shetld*	C2	40
West Tarbert *Strath*	E1	11
West Thirston *Northum*	F1	9
West Woodburn *Northum*	D2	9
West Woodside *Cumbr*	B3	8
Wester Causewayend *Lothn*	E2	13
Westerdale *Highl*	B2	38
Westerhope *T. & W.*	F2	9
Westerton *Grampn*	C3	32
Westfield *Highl*	A1	38
Westfield *Lothn*	E1	13
Westhill *Grampn*	D2	25
Westlinton *Cumbr*	B3	8
Westmuir *Tays*	B4	24
Westness *Orkney*	B2	39
Westnewton *Cumbr*	A4	8
Westport *Strath*	D3	11
Westrigg *Lothn*	D1	13
Westruther *Borders*	C2	14
Wetheral *Cumbr*	B3	8
Whalton *Northum*	F2	9
Whauphill *D. & G.*	C3	6
Wheen *Tays*	B3	24
Whelpo *Cumbr*	B4	8
Wheyrigg *Cumbr*	A3	8
Whickham *T. & W.*	F3	9
Whigstreet *Tays*	E1	19
Whim *Borders*	F2	13
Whinnow *Cumbr*	B3	8
Whitburn *Lothn*	E1	13
Whitebridge *Highl*	C1	22
Whiteburn *Borders*	B2	14
Whitecairns *Grampn*	E1	25
Whitecastle *Strath*	E3	13
Whitecrook *D. & G.*	B3	6
Whiteface *Highl*	D1	31
Whitehall *Orkney*	C2	39
Whitehills *Grampn*	C2	32
Whitehouse *Grampn*	C1	24
Whitehouse *Strath*	E2	11
Whitekirk *Lothn*	F4	19
Whiteness *Shetld*	B3	40
Whiterashes *Grampn*	E1	25
Whitestone *Grampn*	C2	24
Whithorn *D. & G.*	C4	6
Whiting Bay *Strath*	F3	11
Whitletts *Strath*	B3	12
Whitsome *Borders*	D2	15
Whittingham *Northum*	E4	15
Whittonstall *Northum*	E3	9
Wick *Highl*	C2	38
Widdrington *Northum*	F1	9
Widdrington Station *Northum*	F1	9
Wide Open *T. & W.*	F2	9
Wigton *Cumbr*	A3	8
Wigtown *D. & G.*	C3	6
Wilkhaven *Highl*	E1	31
Wilkieston *Lothn*	F1	13
Willington *Durham*	F4	9
Wilsontown *Strath*	E2	13
Winchburgh *Lothn*	E1	13
Windhill *Highl*	C3	30
Windygates *Fife*	D3	19
Winscales *Cumbr*	F4	7
Wintercleuch *Strath*	E4	13
Wishaw *Strath*	D2	13
Wiston *Strath*	E3	13
Witton Gilbert *Durham*	F4	9
Witton le Wear *Durham*	F4	9
Wolfclyde *Strath*	E3	13
Wolsingham *Durham*	E4	9
Woodham *Durham*	F4	9
Woodhaven *Fife*	E2	19
Woodhead *Grampn*	D3	25
Woodhead *Grampn*	D4	33
Woodland *Durham*	E4	9
Woodlands *D. & G.*	A2	8
Woodside *D. & G.*	F2	7
Woodside *Tays*	D1	19
Wooler *Northum*	D3	15
Workington *Cumbr*	F4	7
Wormiston *Borders*	F2	13
Wormit *Fife*	E2	19
Wyng *Orkney*	A4	39
Wyvis Lodge *Highl*	C2	30
Yarrow *Borders*	A3	14
Yarrow Feus *Borders*	A3	14
Yetts of Muckart *Central*	C3	18
Yieldshields *Strath*	D2	13
Ythanbank *Grampn*	D3	33